Land Use *and* Planning *and* Your Business

Land Use *and* Planning *and* Your Business

Susan Curran and David McDonald

London: The Stationery Office

A CIP catalogue record for this book is available from the British Library.

A Library of Congress CIP catalogue record has been applied for

First published 2001
ISBN 0 11 702705 7

ACKNOWLEDGEMENTS

We owe grateful thanks to four individuals who read part or all of the draft text of this book and made very helpful comments: Keir Hounsome, Head of Law for Norfolk County Council, Neil Parke, Head of Building Control for Norwich City Council, and Councillors Julian Swainson and Eamonn Burgess of Norwich City Council. Responsibility for any remaining errors is, of course, ours.

Susan Curran
David McDonald
June 2001

Published by The Stationery Office Limited
and available from:

The Publications Centre
(Mail, telephone and fax orders only)
PO Box 276, London SW8 5DT
General enquiries 020 7873 0011
Telephone orders 020 7873 9090
Fax orders 020 7873 8200

The Stationery Office Bookshops
123 Kingsway, London WC2B 6PQ
020 7242 6393 Fax 020 7242 6394
68-69 Bull Street, Birmingham B4 6AD
0121 236 9696 Fax 0121 236 9699
33 Wine Street, Bristol BS1 2BQ
0117 9264306 Fax 0117 9294515
9-21 Princess Street, Manchester M60 8AS
0161 834 7201 Fax 0161 833 0634
16 Arthur Street, Belfast BT1 4GD
028 9023 8451 Fax 028 9023 5401
The Stationery Office Oriel Bookshop
18-19 High Street, Cardiff CF1 2BZ
029 2039 5548 Fax 029 2038 4347
71 Lothian Road, Edinburgh EH3 9AZ
0870 606 5566 Fax 0870 606 5588

Accredited Agents
(See Yellow Pages)

and through good booksellers

Printed in the UK by The Stationery Office Limited
TJ0005463 C8 10/01 655211 19585.

Contents

Route map

Do you primarily want to know:

- whether you need planning permission?
  Chapter 3 gives you core guidance.

- how to make a planning application?
  Chapter 2 gives you background information.
  Chapter 4 covers the detail of preparing your application.
  Chapter 6 explains how the application is handled.

- how planning policy will affect your business?
  Chapters 1 and 2 explain the general issues.
  Chapter 5 and 8 cover specific issues.

- about building regulations?
  Chapter 7 provides an overview.

- what to do if you have contravened planning regulations?
  Chapter 9 explains the planning enforcement process.

- how to protest about other people's development proposals?
  Chapter 10 explains how to object to planning applications and structure plan proposals.

Introduction

WHY WE HAVE WRITTEN THIS BOOK

Land-use and planning issues come to the fore for busy managers when they need to *plan for development:* to change the use of existing buildings, to have extensions to them designed and built, or to relocate or expand onto a new site. There are a complex net of legal requirements which you need to meet, and the better you understand them, the easier you will find it to meet them. At times like these, you need a guide to get you started; to give you an overview of the complex professional fields into which you will be stepping, and to tell you how and where to get advice and help.

However, planning and land-use issues don't only affect businesses when they are planning land-use developments. The business environment in which you work is shaped all the time by *planning policy made by government and planning decisions made by local authorities.* If you understand how those decisions are made – and how you can play your part in influencing them – then you will be in a better position to plan the development of your own business in a way which fits, and does not conflict with, the planning framework of your neighbourhood, your town or city, and your region.

Your neighbours' planning proposals also affect you, and often when you least want

them to. You need to know how to find out about them, and what to do if you are unhappy about them.

Finally, you need to understand the *broader context of sustainable development* in which your business operates; not only because it shapes the policy framework, but because it helps your business operate in a modern and sustainable way, for today and for the future.

WHO THIS BOOK IS FOR

This book is aimed primarily at managers in small and medium-sized enterprises, who do not have in-house advice available when trying to manage their changing business in a changing environment. Some of the material is specific to commercial enterprises, but most of it is also applicable to those managing or controlling public-sector and other types of operation. Managers in larger companies may also find that it provides a useful overview of land-use and planning issues.

The book will also be useful to others who need to understand the planning context, including students in land-use related fields, local councillors and private individuals.

The book deals with the planning system in the United Kingdom, although it briefly sets this system within a wider international

1

perspective. Many aspects of the planning system are the same in England, Scotland, Wales and Northern Ireland. The core information given here applies primarily to England, but we try to point out where legislation and practice differ in other parts of the UK.

WHAT YOU WILL GET OUT OF READING THIS BOOK

Primarily, we hope that this book will provide a first stop for those new to the planning process. It will give you guidelines for what you need to do if you are:

- considering a development
- preparing a planning application
- affected by a neighbour's development proposals
- concerned about wider land-use developments that affect your business
- or facing enforcement action by your local planning authority.

A short guide like this cannot, of course, be an adequate alternative to good professional advice. Nor is it an authoritative summary of planning law; to do that would take several large volumes. However, we hope we will succeed in giving you an overview of the field, and in telling you what kind of advice you need, when you need it, and where to find it.

Land-use issues *and* why they matter

This chapter aims to set the context for the detailed information on planning policy and practice that follows. Once you have read it you should have a general understanding of:

- why sustainable development is important nationally and internationally
- the role of land-use planning in a wider policy of sustainable development
- the advantages of good land-use planning and the careful planning of building developments to your business.

SUSTAINABLE DEVELOPMENT

Sustainable development is one of the core tenets of development thinking on a world-wide scale, but it is not easy to define. Perhaps the best known definition is that it is development which aims to meet the needs of today without compromising the prospects of future generations. As such, it is clearly a priority on a highly developed planet with limited natural resources. It is a specific feature of policy frameworks on a local, regional, national, European and global scale and therefore plays a large part in setting the scene within which individual commercial and other developments take place.

As the UK government defines and imple-ments the policy of sustainable development, it has four core principles:

- the maintenance of high and stable levels of economic growth and employment
- social progress which recognises the needs of everyone
- effective protection of the environment
- prudent use of natural resources.

These resources are reflected in the land-use planning system, as in many other aspects of government policy.

SUSTAINABLE CONSTRUCTION

A part of the government's broader policy of

3

sustainable development is concerned with sustainable construction. This is concerned with making certain that buildings are constructed in line with sustainability objectives, ensuring that they are:

- safe and secure
- economical in their use of raw materials
- economical in their use of energy
- built in a way that avoids or minimises pollution
- designed and built with their entire life-cycle in mind, including eventual demolition and reinstatement of the site where this is appropriate.

It is worth keeping in mind these objectives when you plan to develop your business, not only because they are government policy, but because they are worthwhile in themselves.

LAND-USE PLANNING

At a practical level, as an individual manager, you may feel that you are concerned primarily with development control; with the system of planning approvals which are required before most types of development and change, both physical and related to land-use, take place. However, development control is only one aspect of the larger activity that is properly known as land-use planning, though it is often referred to more simply as 'planning' (used in many places throughout this book), and is sometimes still known by its more outdated name of 'town planning', or even 'town and country planning'.

Land-use planning is a function of central, regional and local government. At the central government level, it is handled primarily by the Department of Transport, Local Government and Regions (DTLR) in England, the Department of the Environment for Northern Ireland, and largely devolved to the Scottish Parliament and Welsh Assembly. In local government, it was until relatively recently handled by planning departments, and is now handled by departments with a wider range of names and functions such as 'environment and development' and 'development and regeneration services'.

Planning is a profession with recognised qualifications, regulated by a professional body, the Royal Town Planning Institute (RTPI). Many of its practitioners work in the public sector, but others work in the private sector as freelance consultants, or on the staff of organisations involved in the development process.

At the core of the planning process is the aim of planning and overseeing a controlled evolution from today's situation to a better future. Planning analyses the available stock of land, buildings and natural resources, takes account of the uses that are already made of them, and seeks to set a framework for future change and development. As such, it is a practical profession, though not without its streak of idealism. It takes fully into account the existing infrastructure and pattern of development, and in general what is already in existence is deemed to be, if not capable of improvement, at least acceptable in principle. But what is already in existence may not be adequate to ensure a sustainable future, and therefore needs development and change in order to take account of lifestyle changes, technological and commercial changes, as well as the inevitable process of decay and renewal. The aim of planning is to ensure that what is of value in the present is conserved; what is needed in the future is provided; and what is created in the future fits in with the ethos of sustainability, and is of as high quality as can realistically be realised.

Among the issues that planners needs to consider are:

- Sustaining the natural character and diversity of different areas, especially the countryside and undeveloped coasts.
- Protecting and enhancing wildlife habitats and species, and promoting biodiversity.
- Protecting the stock of agricultural land, both arable and grazing.
- Conserving the historically evolved landscape.
- Conserving (or where this is not practicable, recording) the archaeological heritage.
- Conserving what is of most value in the built environment.
- Conserving and developing the public infrastructure (roads, rail and other transport systems, water supply, sewerage and drainage, power supply, telecommunication systems, facilities such as schools and hospitals and so on).
- Controlling new physical development in ways that enhance both the natural landscape and the built environment.
- Ensuring that adequate supplies of land are available for all essential purposes (transport, public services, employment uses, housing, agriculture and so on).
- Ensuring that private development makes good use of the existing infrastructure and conforms with the pattern in which it develops.
- Ensuring that development of all kinds respects the needs and rights of existing land users.
- Ensuring that natural resources (water, energy sources and building materials) are exploited efficiently and sustainably, both during and after the construction process.
- Ensuring that energy is used efficiently in industry, in heating and lighting buildings, in transport usage and for other purposes.

- Improving the quality of the air, soil and water, and controlling possible sources of pollution.
- Limiting the degree of noise and light pollution.
- Bringing contaminated and derelict land and buildings back into productive use.
- Enhancing the quality of life for all.
- Resolving disputes, and ensuring fairness between competing interests.

ISSUES THAT ARE NOT THE CONCERN OF THE PLANNING PROCESS

Our interest here is predominantly with land-use planning, but this is only one aspect of the planning for future development with which both businesses and individuals need to concern themselves. In a broad sense, businesses have to plan how they will finance future development, how they will retain and develop their customer base, how they will retain and develop their staff base, and so on. Even in the context of planning for physical development (for example, the change of use of an existing building, extension to or alteration of existing buildings, or the choice of site for, and design of, an entirely new factory, warehouse, office or retail outlet), many issues have to be considered that are beyond the scope of the land-use planning process. These include, for example, the need to ensure adequate supplies of raw materials, both for the building process and for the business in its changed state, and to ensure that processes subject to statutory control (such as industrial processes giving rise to pollution or waste) are designed and operated in accordance with all statutory requirements. These wider issues are not dealt with in this book. However, throughout the book we try to explain when other types of permission may be required in order to facilitate development. Planners are not directly responsible for developing land uses; they are responsible for setting a framework for their development. They might designate land as suitable for a new hospital development, for example, but they would not obtain funding for the hospital, design its buildings or oversee its construction (except to the degree necessary to ensure that it conforms to the plans approved). Public development is the concern of other government departments and functions. Private development is the concern of private developers. The modern trend is for planners to take a proactive stance: to anticipate, to encourage, and to suggest; but they still do not develop, they merely set out the framework for development. A planning officer in a local authority might draw up a brief suggesting what mix of uses would be acceptable on a site that has become available for development purposes. He or she might go a little further and analyse the constraints that were hindering development, suggesting ways of overcoming them, but the planning officer cannot and would not tell a private individual or a public body how they *must* develop, only how they would be *permitted* to develop. (However, in some cases the planner can insist that repair work *is* carried out.)

Where your business is concerned, it is important to understand that the primary concern of planners is with land-use issues, not with economic issues. It is legitimate for planners to anticipate how many jobs will be needed for the workers in their area, what types of enterprise might provide them, and where those enterprises might acceptably be located; how many new houses will be needed, and what land should be designated for possible housing development; how many shops will be required, and what pattern of large and small commercial centres would be appropriate. The role of the planner will, only to a very peripheral extent, include analysing whether a developer will make money from building and selling new homes, or whether a business will profitably be able to set up and run a new factory or office. This is *your* job, if you are looking to act as a developer. The planner does not normally ask whether an applicant for planning permission is in a position to fund the proposed development, as this is not the concern of the planning process. As the applicant, you need to work out how to achieve this. However, there are some contexts in which economic issues are considered: for example, if a number of competing proposals, perhaps for leisure or shopping complexes, were submitted simultaneously, the planning authority would work to ensure that no more than a reasonably viable number were approved and implemented.

Planning pays some regard to rights of existing land users from a land-use perspective (though these rights are limited: it will not, for example, protect a home-owner whose view is affected by a new development); but it does not exist to protect existing economic interests. The proprietor of an existing corner shop cannot prevent a new supermarket from being built on the grounds that it will take away trade; a land owner cannot stop a new development by another person that reduces the value of existing property. Generally, government policy is that planning should not act to restrict competition, but rather to encourage it.

Planning is not primarily about individuals: it is about land and the use that is made of land. Planning permission generally (though with occasional exceptions) dictates what can be done on a specific site, not what can be done by a specific individual.

Even when it comes to physical aspects of development, the interest of planners is restricted. Their concern is primarily with the public face of the individual development, not its private face. Planners can refuse development that is visually out of keeping with its setting, whether in scale, in design, or in choice of materials, but they are not usually concerned with whether the internal layout of a building is acceptable. However, some internal design aspects are controlled by the related (but separate) field of building control, as are other aspects of the building process that are not within the scope of land-use planning, such as the stability of the construction and the quality of building workmanship.

Finally, only in a broad sense is the planning process concerned with the use of buildings. Here again, planners are looking at how the use affects the outside world, rather than how it is organised internally. Planners grant or refuse permission on the basis of broad use classes, such as shops, or general industrial uses (see page 23); they do not concern themselves with the minutiae of how buildings are used or businesses operate within those classes.

WHY LAND-USE ISSUES ARE IMPORTANT FOR BUSINESSES

It is important for virtually every enterprise – and every individual household – to take careful account both of the choice of its location, and of the design of the buildings in that location. In a real sense, the planning process is a boon to business, because its statutory require

ments help to ensure that development is carefully considered from many different viewpoints.

It is vital for a business to locate itself in the right place. The location of the business will, for example:

- Affect the transport requirements generated by the business. It will determine how far, and by what methods and routes, raw materials are brought to the location. It will determine how far and by what method goods (or suppliers of services) must travel in order to reach customers. It will also dictate the pattern of staff travel to work.

- Affect the ability of the business to advertise or otherwise to attract custom: a shop on a busy street with plenty of passing trade will fare differently from one on a quiet backstreet, where the only customers who come are those who consciously seek it out.

- Have a variety of effects on neighbouring land users. For example, a shop that is located in an existing or developing commercial centre will benefit from the 'drawing' effect of other nearby businesses, regardless of whether they offer competing or complementary goods, while a shop in an isolated location will not benefit in this way. A factory or farming activity which generates noxious smells will negatively affect its neighbours, so is best kept away from housing and other people-intensive land uses; but an office with a high-density workforce might better be located close to residents who might provide that workforce.

- Have an impact on the image of the business: a smart city-centre office with a high rent, for example, conveys a different message from a basic unit on an industrial estate.

- Have a long-term impact as the wider pattern of land usage and infrastructure develops: so that, for example, a shop in a declining commercial area is likely to face a different future from one in an 'action area' into which investment is being directed, or a newly created retail park.

Careful choice of the building design is also vital. The design of the building, and its location on the site, for example, will affect:

- the way in which the building functions, and the overall efficiency, or otherwise, of the operations within it
- the efficiency with which other land on the site can be utilised
- the energy efficiency of the building
- the security of the building
- the building's lifespan and maintenance requirements
- the way in which the building and business is perceived by others, including customers, suppliers and staff.

WHY AWARENESS OF PLANNING IS VITAL FOR BUSINESS

No business looks to develop without an appreciation of why that development makes sense: whether the reason is an old and inefficient building that needs replacing, a change in technology that requires different premises, or the overall expansion or contraction of the business. However, businesses that develop successfully also have two broader needs. First, and perhaps most obviously, they need an understanding of the legal and policy framework within which development takes place, so they can make their own plans in conformance with the requirements of the land-use planning system. Second, small as well as large businesses today have to be aware of their social responsibilities and to practise environmental management – sustain-able development, if you like, on the scale of the individual enterprise. The planning system provides a framework which encourages them to do so.

Awareness of planning policy and regulations is important because:

- It will help you to be aware, in a general sense, of the options that are available for the development of your business.
- Future strategic plans – what is designated as acceptable for adjoining buildings, your immediate neighbourhood, your town or city and region, the country as a whole – will have an impact on your business, whatever its nature. They will shape changing patterns of commercial activity, potential new competition, staff availability, and so on.
- If you are looking to alter or extend existing buildings, you will be able to do so most effectively and efficiently if you are aware right at the outset what is likely to be acceptable, and what is certain not to be.
- Similarly, if you are looking to relocate or to expand onto another site, the planning system can direct you straight away to the sites where your type of use would be acceptable, taking into account the likelihood of development proving acceptable on the sites that are physically available.
- Conformance with the law is vital, because of the downside in financial cost and lost time (which includes fines and other penalties, the risk of work being wasted, and adverse publicity) of any failure to adhere to the regulations.

A more general awareness of sustainable development and its requirements is essential because:

- Sustainable development on a worldwide scale is vital to the quality of life, and each individual and enterprise has a part to play in achieving it.

- A reputation for environmentally responsible behaviour enhances the image of any enterprise, large or small, encourages customers and improves the morale of staff.
- Environmentally responsible operations tend to be efficient operations, reducing both energy costs and more general operating costs. Sometimes there is a capital cost to pay, but it is frequently repaid in revenue savings.
- Increasingly, the regulatory system is putting costs onto enterprises which harm the environment, and rewarding those which act in an environmentally beneficial way.

KEY POINTS

✔ *Sustainable development is the key phrase that dictates the pattern of development on every scale from the individual to the global.*

✔ *If you're looking to develop your business in any way which affects its buildings and land-use generally, it is essential to be aware of the land-use planning function. Even if you are not looking to carry out a specific development, you will be more successful in sustaining your business if you appreciate the environment within which it operates.*

✔ *At the level of the individual development, the land-use planning system is known as development control.*

✔ *Land-use planning is only one aspect of the many types of planning that underpin a successful development.*

✔ *One land-use aspect of successful development is the choice of the right site for your business.*

✔ *The other major aspect is finding the right design for the building on that site.*

✔ *A successful development is one which fits the overall philosophy of sustainable development: it is best for the planet, and best for your business.*

CHAPTER 2

Planning: an overview

In Chapter 1, we introduced the general concepts of sustainable development and land-use planning. This chapter outlines how the system operates in practice.

By the end of this chapter you should be aware:

- in broad terms, what planning policy comprises and how it interacts with planning permission
- how international and European, national, regional and local plans interact to provide a framework of planning policy
- how planning policy helps to determine whether your planning application will be granted
- of the benefits and drawbacks of the system, especially as they affect small and medium-sized enterprises.

PLANNING PERMISSION AND PLANNING POLICY

As we explained in Chapter 1, development control – the business of considering, and granting or refusing, applications for planning permission – is only one aspect of the broad field of land-use planning. Much of the rest of the field is concerned with developing the policy framework in which applications for planning permissions are considered and determined.

Planning permission

Planning permission, sometimes referred to as planning consent or planning approval, is concerned with two different, but interrelated, things:

- What physical works can be carried out on a piece of land: what buildings can be erected, how existing buildings can be altered, whether mineral excavation can take place, and so on.
- What types of activity can take place on the land and in its buildings: for example, whether it can be used for offices, a factory, a warehouse, a shop or a block of flats.

Most existing land uses and buildings already have planning permission, or have been in operation so long that they are regarded as lawful and therefore do not need permission. When you make a planning application and it is granted, you receive a written notice of permission. We explore later in the book what land-use activities already have planning permission, how to find out what is permitted on a site, and how to apply for planning permission when you need to do so.

A new grant of planning permission gives the applicant permission from a land-use perspective to develop or use the land in the way specified. It must be implemented within a fixed length of time (normally five years) and if this is not done, the permission lapses, unless it is formally renewed. Once the permission has been implemented – the building built, or the use put into practice – the permission is permanent, unless it has been specifically time-limited as a *condition* of the permission.

Planning permission normally applies to a site, not to an applicant (although there are exceptions: see page 47). Once the permission has been granted, anyone with the legal right to do so can implement that permission. If you are the owner of the site, you can sell it and the permission remains with the site and can be implemented by the purchaser (provided there is no legal hindrance). As applicant, you cannot transfer the permission to another site: so permission to carry on a fish-canning business on site A does not give you the right to carry on that business on any other site; permission to erect a building of an agreed design on site B does not give you permission to erect the same building on any other site. Sometimes permission to use the site for a specific purpose may be granted, but made conditional on its use by a specific individual or organisation; but it is not automatically personal to the *applicant*.

The planning system works in a way that is evolutionary, rather than revolutionary. Normally, buildings that are already on a site can stay there; activities that are being carried out on a site can be continued (unless permission was granted for a limited period which has expired). This is, of course, from a planning viewpoint: there's always the possibility that other legislation might make it illegal to continue to do something that was formerly allowed. However, if one building is demolished it does not automatically follow that a replacement building, even a very similar replacement, will be acceptable. If one use ended long ago, it does not automatically follow that its resumption will be acceptable. There may be a presumption that this will be the case, but there is no guarantee of it; and if a temporary permission expires, it certainly does not always follow that it will be renewed.

RIGHTS AND PERMISSIONS

Permission from a land-use perspective should not be confused with a *right* to develop the site. It is only one of the rights that is required in order to do this. Planning permission does not give you ownership of the site, the right to override the legal interests of others (such as existing tenants) in the site and the buildings on it, the right to ignore covenants which restrict use of the site, or the right to circumvent legal controls on the activities you might carry out. It is up to you, as the applicant, to ensure that you have the legal right before implementing planning permission, and to ensure that you have all necessary approvals and authorisations: building control certificates, alcohol or entertainment licences, water abstraction permits, pollution control permits, or whatever else may apply in your particular circumstances.

Planning policy

Applications for planning permission for specific developments are assessed within a broader framework which is made up of two types of planning policy:

- First, there are overall policies covering the way in which acceptable development can and should take place. These might dictate, for example, the amount of new housing that is required in a specific region, the proportion of land that needs to be allocated for other uses (such as heavy industry) or the types of building material that are preferred in a sensitive area such as the centre of a historic town. They also provide guidelines on issues such as the amount of parking provision that is allowable with a new development, and the requirements for safe road access.

- Second, there are geographical policies. These are related to specific sites, areas or regions, and indicate which kinds of development will be acceptable in which places. They cover both the infrastructure (for example, where new roads are to be built or new settlements established) and the type of use (for example, exactly what land is allocated for housing use, and what for retail and commercial use). So the overall policy for a region might identify a need for 5,000 new dwellings, and the geographical policy for the local planning areas within that region will identify areas within settlement boundaries where applications for housing development will be acceptable (provided they meet all other acceptability criteria).

Both overall and geographical policies take account of the fact that, in general, there is considerable competition for development land in the UK, especially in England (and even more particularly in South-East England). England has a population of nearly 50 million, and its total land area is only about 4 per cent of the EU total. About half the land in England is not available for development, either because it is already built up, or because it comprises protected areas such as green belts and Areas of Outstanding Natural Beauty (AONBs). It is an important role of the land-use planning function to ensure that the available land is allocated in such a way that development is kept broadly in balance: for instance, it would not be desirable for a large number of houses to be built in an area where insufficient land was available either for businesses which could provide employment for the new population, or for public services such as schools and hospitals.

BENEFITS OF THE PLANNING PROCESS FOR BUSINESSES

Sometimes business people regard the planning system as a major disadvantage, both because the system of making planning applications is expensive and bureaucratic, and because the policy of allocating areas of land for specific purposes inevitably tends to restrict some forms of development, and to drive up the prices of land for which there is a high demand compared to the allocation. However, it is important for you to realise that, in fact, the planning system has very real benefits for businesses large and small and, indeed, for individuals as well.

- The existence of a clearly specified framework helps to ensure that overall, development is more coherent and successful than if it took place in a piecemeal manner.
- The framework applies to the public infrastructure as well as to private developments, so it is possible for private developers to plan in a way that will be in step with the developing infrastructure.
- Because the framework is public and applies to all developers, business or

personal, it provides a secure basis for a land and property market.

- It is possible for you, as an actual and potential land-user, to find out what the policies are for your area, and to make your plans and commit to investment confidently in the context of those policies. You do not need to waste resources working up plans that have little hope of acceptance.

- Since you know other developments will also have to comply with the guidelines, you can have a clear sense of how your business will fit into the wider pattern of development in your region, and can plan for future development accordingly.

- The planning system tries to ensure that land uses mesh together in an acceptable way, and that 'bad neighbour' uses are kept separate from people-intensive uses. You can be reasonably confident that a 'bad neighbour' development such as a landfill tip or chemical factory will not be permitted right next to your existing 'clean' business premises or home.

- Finally, because the process of drawing up policies is public and democratic, you have the opportunity to provide input as a consultee, at several different levels.

CONSTRAINTS AND DRAWBACKS OF THE PLANNING PROCESS

However, there is no gain without pain, and it remains true that the planning system does put constraints on businesses, creates its full share of red tape, and represents a real cost to businesses.

PLANNING APPLICATIONS

It is estimated (by the DTLR) that in England there are around 1.5 million businesses, which together submit about 100,000 business planning applications each year.

- Fees are charged for most planning applications, and these cost businesses in England cumulatively about £100 million a year. Some businesses also enter into planning agreements (see Chapter 4) which oblige them to pay for improvements to the infrastructure and similar off-site developments, as a condition of obtaining planning permission. The cost of these is harder to quantify, but the DTLR has estimated that in total, they could add another £100 million to the cost to business of the planning system.

- Limitations on the permitted use of land increase competition where the permitted use is in short supply and, in consequence, raise land prices and rents. Research suggests that the sectors most affected by these limitations are new-build housing and the retail sector. The limitation is also most clearly felt in areas of comparatively strong growth, especially South-East England, but also in the North West and West Midlands conurbations.

- Since restrictions on residential land tend to raise house prices, this leads to a demand for higher wages, and thus indirectly puts higher costs on businesses.

- The planning process can be slow, and unless applications are made well before the intended date of starting a development, this acts as a drag on the pace of development. The government's target is that 80 per cent of district planning applications should be determined within eight weeks, but in the last quarter of 2000 only about 62 per cent were determined within this time limit. If an application is refused, and the applicant chooses to submit a revised application or to make an appeal, then the process is considerably slower.

THE FRAMEWORK OF PLANNING POLICY

In this section of the chapter we outline the

main elements that combine to create a framework for planning policy. Regulations, policies and commitments at every level, have an impact on what is allowable for each individual development. So, dull as this framework may seem, it is important that you understand how it operates.

The government's general principle is that the planning framework should be operated from the 'bottom up', broadly in line with the EC principle of subsidiarity, so that only those projects which have a more than local significance are subject to determination at a higher than local level. Here, however, we review the broader international framework first, so as to provide a sense of the larger issues which shape the planning picture, before moving down to the local and neighbourhood scale.

At the highest level, the UK's international commitments under international agreements, particularly those regarding climate change and the control of pollution, are a major force in encouraging sustainable development, and a major factor in limiting what development can take place, and how it should be carried out.

Until recently, the EC was not a major player in the specific field of land-use planning, though a variety of EC laws and regulations have an impact on the type of planning framework that has been developed. Over the last few years, EC initiatives have, however, played a part in shaping the national planning system.

Within the UK, there is input to planning policy at the national level, where policy is primarily strategic rather than geographical; at the regional level, which is taking on increas-

ing importance both strategically and geographically; and at each level of local government, where structure plans and local plans shape in detail the geographical and policy framework, and where local planning authorities (LPAs) carry policy down in some cases to the individual site level.

THE POLICY FRAMEWORK

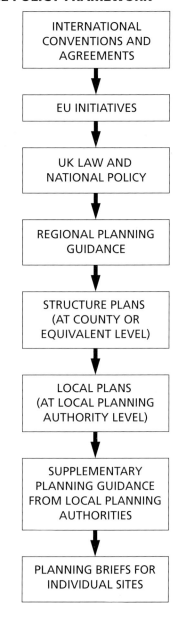

INTERNATIONAL CONVENTIONS AND AGREEMENTS

EU INITIATIVES

UK LAW AND NATIONAL POLICY

REGIONAL PLANNING GUIDANCE

STRUCTURE PLANS (AT COUNTY OR EQUIVALENT LEVEL)

LOCAL PLANS (AT LOCAL PLANNING AUTHORITY LEVEL)

SUPPLEMENTARY PLANNING GUIDANCE FROM LOCAL PLANNING AUTHORITIES

PLANNING BRIEFS FOR INDIVIDUAL SITES

Sustainable development on an international scale

A large number of different bodies are involved in sustainable development on an international scale, but in terms of specific commitments that affect land-use planning, perhaps the most significant is the UN Framework Convention on Climate Change (UNFCCC). This developed from the 1992 Rio Conference on Environment and Development, and has led to a number of international agreements to limit emission of chemicals which contribute to global warming and to the destruction of the ozone layer. (These issues are discussed in detail in *The Climate Change Levy and Your Business,* a companion book to this title.) These include chemicals that are emitted through processes that generate and use energy, and in consequence there is pressure on the UK government – as on other countries worldwide – to reduce its energy generation, as well as to move to 'cleaner' forms of energy, and to make other land-use changes such as the provision of 'carbon sinks', areas of woodland or other intense vegetation which absorb carbon dioxide, a significant pollutant. Other substances that do not affect the ozone layer are nevertheless serious pollutants, and there are also international initiatives to reduce the use and emission of these, and thus to bring about cleaner air, water and less polluted soil.

It could be argued that much of the development that is carried out today is not truly 'sustainable' in a purist sense. Many developments demand resources that are not readily renewable, both in construction and in operation, and may have other negative effects on the environment, such as an increase in air pollution. However governments tend to be pragmatic: they rarely interpret sustainable development as equalling non-development. As a result, there is not generally a question of new commercial initiatives being rejected purely *because* they will be significant users of energy or generators of pollution. However, there are presumptions:

- that new (or relocating) enterprises of all kinds will be located in places which minimise the amount of transport flow generated, and thus reduce the amount of pollution caused directly or indirectly by that transport
- that enterprises will be located in places which encourage the use of less polluting forms of transport (foot, cycle and public transport) and discourage the use of more polluting forms, such as the private car
- that new buildings will be designed as far as possible to be energy-efficient in their heating, lighting and other services
- that industrial and commercial processes will also be designed to be energy-efficient
- that industrial and commercial processes will be designed and operated so as to minimise pollution
- and that enterprises will be designed, and operated, in ways that minimise the production of waste, and the consequent difficulties of disposing of it.

Some of these issues are addressed directly by the land-use planning process, and others are the concern primarily of other forms of regulation such as Integrated Pollution Prevention and Control.

EU initiatives

The European Spatial Development Perspective is a recent intergovernmental initiative which is aimed at providing a framework for land-use planning decisions within the EU. At this stage it is not binding on the governments of member states, but it is an early stage in the general move to bring about harmonisation in

15

planning policies, and it seems likely that in the future, there will be further moves in this direction.

A number of more specific EU initiatives also have a significant effect on the planning systems of member states. The Trans-European Network, for example, is an initiative to create an integrated network, not only for transport, but also for energy transmission, telecommunications and other aspects of the infrastructure. INTERREG 11 C (Community Initiative on Transnational Co-operation on Spatial Planning) is a specifically spatial planning initiative, which is designed to promote transnational co-operation on land-use planning. Three recent programmes have had a particular impact on the UK: those covering the North Sea Region, the North West Metropolitan Area and the Atlantic Area. (More information on these and other initiatives is available from the EU website, accessible from www.europa/eu/int/)

The UK national planning framework

In geographical terms, surprisingly little planning is done on a national basis. There are powers for Parliament to grant planning permission through a Special Development Order or by a hybrid bill, but although these could in theory be used for projects of national importance, in practice this is not often done, and planning permission for the vast majority of projects is handled through the relevant local planning authority. Recent government consultation documents have acknowledged this as a weakness of the national system, and it may be that in the future there will be a greater trend towards scrutiny on a national scale of projects with national significance.

Planning law is of course implemented on a national scale, though as with other aspects of national law, there is (and is likely to continue to be) an increasing influence from EU law and regulations. A number of Acts of Parliament shape the statutory planning system, of which the most important is the Town and Country Planning Act 1990. (Other significant pieces of legislation are listed in 'Further Reading' on page 94.)

From a policy perspective too, there is a well-established framework of national planning policy which provides guidance for local planning authorities. Much of the policy is incorporated in a series of *Planning Policy Guidance (PPG)* notes. The main ones are again listed in 'Further Reading'. They can be accessed through the DTLR website (www.planning.dtlr.gov.uk/) or are available for sale via The Stationery Office.

As well as the DTLR, a number of government agencies and other national bodies have an impact on planning policy, and also on the determination of individual planning applications, for which many of them are statutory consultees. The Environment Agency, for example, provides feedback to local authorities on the impact of developments on flood risk, not only for the development itself, but for the area as a whole. It also agrees 25-year plans for maintaining water supplies with individual water companies, and this water-supply framework filters down to have an impact on structure plans, local plans, and on the determination of applications which will affect water demand. The Highways Agency has input when developments are likely to impact upon the traffic flow on trunk roads; English Heritage comments when an application affects a listed building or scheduled ancient monument, and so on.

Regional planning

The structure of regional government in England is still under active review and development, and the role and structure of regional planning, too, is in flux at present. A revised draft was issued in 1999 of the PPG on *Regional Planning*, though the new system has yet to be implemented at the time of writing (early 2001).

Most regional planning is carried out for regions which are synonymous with those covered by Government Offices for the Regions (GORs), though there are exceptions in Eastern and South-East England. The outcome of the regional planning process is *Regional Planning Guidance (RPG)*, which is developed by regional planning bodies working in association with businesses and other regional stakeholders. The draft guidance they produce is subject to consultations before endorsement by the Secretary of State. At present RPG is non-statutory: it provides a general framework for statutory development plans which are drawn up at more local levels, and carries weight when it comes to determining planning applications.

Regional planning bodies have, up to now, consisted of regional conferences of the relevant local planning authorities, but they may in future turn to regional chambers set up under the Regional Development Agencies Act 1998, which will include at least 30 per cent of members not drawn from local government. There is a real opportunity here for businesses who are interested to shape the pattern of regional planning (and thus influence the pattern of their own development on a regional scale) to become involved.

Among the general aims of RPG, which looks set to become more significant in the future, are:

- to provide a broad strategy for development in the region
- to determine the general location of regionally or sub-regionally significant development, which could, for example, include major new retail centres and major new factories
- to set out an integrated transport strategy, which will of course interact with integrated transport strategies at the national and European level, and
- to provide a framework to assist with bids for EU resources (which are, of course, of great importance to many businesses).

Below regional level

In England, local government varies in structure from area to area, and the allocation of planning responsibilities reflects these various patterns. Where there are two tiers of local government (typically county and district councils), the county level is responsible for drawing up strategic *structure plans* and policies for mineral extraction and waste handling, and the district for drawing up less strategic and more geographically based *local plans*. In London, other metropolitan areas and a few non-metropolitan areas which have unitary local government, a *unitary development plan* combines the functions of structure and local plans, and includes minerals and waste policies.

National Park authorities also play a role in planning policy in their own areas.

In London, the Mayor has responsibilities for the preparation of a 'spatial development strategy' (SDS).

Structure plans

Structure plans drawn up at the county level or its equivalent, have until now been the main tool for planning development on a strategic level, but as regional planning bodies become more established, this role may diminish in importance. The structure plans take account, of course, of the policy and legislative framework that is imposed from above. They consider social, economic and environmental factors, and are expected to take account of the likely resources available: in other words, they are plans for what can reasonably be expected to happen, and not for an unrealisable idea.

If your business is looking to develop on a significant scale, you will need to be aware of what is in your area's structure plan. You can buy a copy of the plan, which normally consists of a key diagram and a written account of policies and proposals, from the planning authority which produced it, or check it out in your local library. It normally looks at least fifteen years ahead, and is revised, in theory, every five years (though in practice, sometimes rather less often).

The structure plan will cover issues such as:

- Plans to develop the area's infrastructure (including, but not limited to the transport infrastructure) and how this is to be integrated with other land uses.
- Target figures for the amount of new housing that is to be built in the area.
- A target for the amount of development that should take place on brownfield (reused) and greenfield (previously undeveloped) sites.
- Details of green belts and other areas where development will be discouraged or prevented.
- Plans to develop the area's economy, and general indications of where industrial, business, retail and other employment-generating and wealth-creating development should take place.
- Conservation issues: of the natural environment, the built environment, the archaeological heritage.
- Plans for future energy generation, including the use of renewable energy sources.
- Plans for waste treatment and disposal.
- Policies and plans for tourism, leisure and recreation.
- Proposals for land reclamation and reuse.

As with other tiers of the planning process, the structure plan is subject to a process of drafting, consultation, review and amendment before it is finally accepted. (See Chapter 10 for more information on providing your own input to your area's structure plan.)

Local plans

Local plans contain more detailed guidance than structure plans, down to the level of proposals for specific sites. These will in many ways be of most importance to you, because however small your planned development is, they provide the detailed framework that tells you whether it is likely to be acceptable. They are developed (through a consultation procedure; again, see Chapter 10) by district authorities and National Park authorities. Usually they consist of text and a map with land-use data, and again they can be bought from the authority which produced them, or consulted in local libraries.

They cover issues such as:

- Defining areas where development is acceptable, using terms such as 'settlement boundary', 'built-up area', 'village envelope' or 'housing framework'.
- Policies for rural areas.
- Detailed guidelines for new housing: its location, types of housing (for example, low-cost or open market), design guidelines and so on.
- Policies on conversion of buildings, for example, for housing use.
- Local standards for building design, which will be applied throughout the local area.
- Specific standards for design in sensitive areas.
- Rules about specific types of development, particularly domestic developments such as house extensions.
- General guidance on how specific sites should be developed.

Supplementary planning guidance (SPG)

This is a general term for guidance issued by local planning authorities which is not part of the local plan. Sometimes it is guidance on issues that arise after the local plan has been adopted, which need to be covered before its next revision; sometimes it is more specific and detailed guidance than is appropriate for the local plan. Common types of SPG include planning briefs for specific sites (see below) and detailed design guidelines for areas of particular sensitivity.

Sometimes SPGs are prepared in consultation with the public and adopted by council resolution. In this case they carry considerable weight in determining planning applications, and in all cases they will carry some weight, so if there is supplementary guidance about the area or site you wish to develop, you should be aware of it. However, SPG does not have the same status as policies in a local or structure plan (or unitary plan), and on occasion it can be overruled.

Planning briefs

A planning brief is a document which provides guidance on the type of development which will be acceptable (or would be preferred) on an individual site. Usually planning briefs are prepared for relatively major sites which become available for development: for example, if a factory closes near a city centre, or a hospital is relocated, and the former site becomes available. Occasionally a brief is prepared for a smaller site that the local planning authority is particularly anxious to see developed, or an area that the local planning authority wants to see regenerated, where it is important to strike a balance between retaining existing buildings of historic or other interest, and encouraging new development.

A planning brief is not a planning application. Nor is it a developer's brief, the term used for a commercial assessment of the value of a site and its development potential. A planning brief is usually prepared by the local planning authority (or by a subcontractor to that authority), though sometimes developers or landowners become involved, or contribute financially to having the brief prepared. The brief provides a framework for gathering information about the site (including, for example, information about the current landowners, particularly if there are a variety of owners and the acquisition of the development land needs to be co-ordinated). Normally the draft brief is discussed by the local planning authority (perhaps in a development control committee meeting: see Chapter 6) and adopted formally, which gives it the status of supplementary planning guidance (discussed above). Reasons for having a brief drawn up might include:

- If the site may be developed by a variety of different developers, and carry a variety of different uses, the planning brief provides a blueprint for all those involved.
- If the site is slow in attracting redevelopment, and the local planning authority wants to kick-start the action, the brief can act as a promotional tool.
- If there are problems about developing a site (perhaps it is land-locked, or the land is contaminated or unstable), the brief can identify ways of overcoming them.
- If the site is to have mixed uses, the brief might indicate where they should be located within the site.
- If design is an important issue, the brief will give design guidelines for the site as a whole.

- If different local authority departments have different aspirations for the site (which might, for example, be owned or part-owned by the authority) the brief resolves their conflicts and provides common advice to developers.

If a site in which you are interested has had a planning brief prepared for it, then it is essential that you consult the brief before developing your proposals in detail and preparing your planning application.

ISSUES THAT AFFECT DECISIONS ON PLANNING APPLICATIONS

All of this policy framework interacts, as we explained earlier in the chapter, to provide the context within which your planning application will be decided. This section of the chapter draws together the issues discussed above and expands on them to outline the issues that are taken into account in considering an individual planning application.

Of course, it is not only important to ensure that your application is approved. It is at least as important to ensure that the development proposal is right for your business, an issue we return to later in the book.

Fit with the policy framework

Do you have to conform absolutely to the plan framework in order to get approval for your planning applications? Not always, but it is a gamble to apply for something that does not fit the framework, and in many cases it will be one that does not pay off. If your proposal deviates from the plan, it will only be approved if there is a good reason for doing so.

POLICY ELEMENTS THAT YOUR PLANNING APPLICATION SHOULD TAKE INTO ACCOUNT

- How it fits national planning guidelines and the wider framework of sustainable development.
- How it fits broad strategic guidelines for your region.
- How it fits the geographical pattern of land-use allocation: is the use you propose the use that has been allocated to your site?
- How it fits design guidance issued by your local planning authority.
- How it fits any planning brief that has been drawn up for the site.

Location issues

The site you nominate for your development will be reviewed carefully by the planning authority. Where review of the site throws up potential problems, of course the planning authority will look to see whether the proposal has recognised them and made provision for overcoming them. Issues that will be taken into account include the following:

- Whether the site is in an area generally appropriate for development.
- Whether the site is in an area of special importance (because of the quality of existing landscape or townscape).
- The ground conditions: whether the land is contaminated, unstable or subject to subsidence.
- Whether the site is subject to flooding, or development of it might cause flooding elsewhere.
- Whether there are public rights of way (which must be retained or adequately relocated by agreement).
- Whether there are existing features which

need to be retained (a significant tree, a drainpipe, etc.)

- The effect of development on existing buildings and existing landscaping, especially features such as trees, hedges and walls.
- Whether there are existing wildlife habitats, especially habitats of rare species which require protecting, either on, or in the vicinity of (and subject to disturbance by development of) the site.
- Whether there are archaeological remains, which may require preservation, or may be excavated and recorded before destruction (see Chapter 8).
- Security issues, and whether development of the site will affect the security of neighbouring buildings.
- Whether the site is generally suitable for the type of use proposed.
- Whether the site is suitable for the physical development in terms of its size, shape and topography (lie of the land).
- Whether essential services (water, drainage, power, telecomms, etc.) are in place.
- Whether service provision above or below ground (for example, underground or above-ground power cables, water and sewage pipes), limits the area of the site that can be developed.
- Whether drainage is adequate.
- Whether road access is adequate.
- Whether the roads in the area can carry any additional traffic that may be generated by the development.
- Whether car-parking provision in the area is adequate.
- How accessible the site is by foot, by cycle and by public transport.
- Generally, what effect development on the site will have on its neighbours.

The design

Design (by which is meant here, not just the shape of the building, but also the materials used for it) is an important planning consideration, but within limits. Of course, local planning authorities want to promote good-quality design, and they will be looking for this in your proposal. The importance of the design will vary from site to site (a site in the centre of an historic town will be seen as more sensitive than a site on a new industrial estate) but wherever the site, the design will need to be in conformance with the general requirements of sustainable development.

The degree to which design can be considered by planners is under review, and the recently formed Commission for Architecture and the Built Environment (CABE) is pressing for greater consideration of the positive values of good design standards.

The proposed building will need to be of an appropriate scale for the site, allowing for the need for landscaping, car parking or other external provision. What scale is appropriate depends in part on the neighbourhood: on a main street in a city centre a new building might well take up almost all the plot available, while in a suburban or urban fringe area it would probably be more appropriate for it to fill only part of the site, leaving room for car parking, landscaping and so on. Similarly, a tall building in an area of predominantly tall buildings would be more acceptable than a tall building in an area of low-rise housing.

The planning authority will also consider where the building is located on the site, and whether the proposed siting is appropriate. There is no general rule for siting buildings: many factors have to be considered, and the appropriate siting will depend entirely on the individual circumstances.

The broad rule is that local planning authorities should not attempt to impose a particular architectural taste or style arbitrarily. They can and should, however, seek to promote or reinforce local distinctiveness. So, if you are proposing to build in an area where the majority of buildings are of local stone, it would be a plus factor if your proposed building was in that material, and a minus if your building was in a stone that had not previously been used in the area.

The planning authority will consider the impact of the development on existing buildings from a design viewpoint, including issues such as:

- whether adequate light is left to the windows of existing buildings. The standard rule is that a 45° angle of light should be left
- whether existing buildings are overlooked, and how this might be overcome (for example, by the use of obscured glass in windows)
- whether the design is visually in keeping with the neighbourhood and fits well with adjoining buildings.

Very detailed features of the design are not strictly a planning consideration, though some planning authorities, particularly those dealing with sensitive areas, may negotiate hard over even very minor design features. The internal design of a building is not generally an issue for land-use planning, and though the planners might comment on it, it should not be a reason for refusal of your application.

Government guidance is that design policies and guidance should focus on encouraging good design, and should avoid stifling responsible innovation, originality and initiative. However, some local councillors responsible for determining planning applications have not yet fully taken this advice on board, and you should be prepared for a battle if your design is particularly unconventional or controversial. It's sometimes helpful if you can point to examples of existing successful buildings (not necessarily in your area, or even in the UK) which are similar in style or conception to your proposal. Passionate advocacy from a well-regarded architect can also help to sway opinion in favour of a proposal.

The use

If you are applying for a change of use alone, then clearly this will be the main consideration; but whatever the content of your planning application, the proposed use of the buildings will be an important issue.

As was mentioned earlier, planning is concerned largely (but not solely) with use classes, i.e., broad categories of usage, within which many changes of specific use are permissible without the need to apply for new permission. However, there are exceptions, so if you are proposing, for example, to move to a building whose current use is significantly different from the one you intend, it is as well not to assume that this will be permissible.

Whatever the proposed use, it needs to be in conformance with plan policies, and also to be appropriate to the immediate neighbourhood: an issue which links with the 'site' issues discussed above, and includes aspects such as the acceptability of additional traffic that might be generated.

USE CLASSES

These are the major broad use classes that are defined in planning legislation. With some exceptions, changes of use that do not cross use-class boundaries do not require planning permission.

A1 Shops, including providers of services which are delivered mostly on the premises via visits from customers: for example, post offices, travel agents, hairdressers, funeral directors and dry cleaners.

A2 Financial and professional services, including banks, building societies and betting shops.

A3 Food and drink: pubs, restaurants, cafes and hot food takeaways.

B1 Business: offices, research and development, and types of light industry that would be appropriate in (though they need not in practice be in) a residential area. This class was introduced in 1987, to allow greater flexibility for businesses to change between light industrial, office and R&D uses, and to place less restriction on 'good neighbour' businesses generally.

B2 General industrial: this includes heavy industry and other types of industry which tend to be 'bad neighbours' because of pollution, noise, smell or other factors.

B8 Storage and distribution, including open air storage.

C1 Hotels, including boarding and guest houses where no significant element of care is provided, but not nursing homes and the like.

C2 Residential institutions: residential care homes, hospitals, nursing homes, boarding schools, residential colleges and training centres.

(continued overleaf)

23

USE CLASSES *(continued)*

C3 Dwelling houses: family houses or houses occupied by up to six residents living as a single household, including those where care is provided for residents. This includes blocks of flats, but not guest houses and hostels.

D1 Non-residential institutions, including surgeries, nurseries, day centres, schools, art galleries, museums, libraries, public halls and churches.

D2 Assembly and leisure: cinemas, concert halls, bingo and dance halls, casinos, swimming baths, skating rinks, gymnasiums and sports arenas (but not including motor sports or sports where firearms are used).

CHANGES OF USE WITHIN THE SAME USE CLASS THAT REQUIRE PLANNING PERMISSION

The most significant of these are material changes of use involving amusement centres, theatres, scrap yards, petrol stations, car showrooms (though these can change to A1 use without permission), taxi and car hire businesses and hostels.

CHANGES OF USE FROM ONE CLASS TO ANOTHER THAT ARE ALLOWED WITHOUT PLANNING PERMISSION

See above for a key to the main use classes. These changes of use are permitted at the time of writing, but they are always subject to change under new legislation, and are sometimes subject to conditions.

Change from:		Change to:
A1 (and a single flat above in mixed use)	to	**A1**
A2	to	**A1** (where the premises have a display window at ground level)
A2 (and a single flat above, where the premises have a display window at ground level)	to	**A1** (where the premises have a display window at ground level)
A2 (and a single flat above in mixed use)		**A2**
Sale of motor vehicles to		**A1**
A3	to	**A1**
A3	to	**A2**
B1 (permission limited to 235 metres of floor space)	to	**B8**
B2	to	**B1**
B2 (permission limited to 235 m^2 of floor space)	to	**B8**
B8 (permission limited to 235 m^2 of floor space)	to	**B1**
A1	to	**A1** plus single flat above
A2	to	**A2** plus single flat above

Planning history

The history of planning applications on the site is a material consideration when you apply for a new permission. If previous permissions of a similar nature have been granted, there is a presumption that your permission will be granted too. This applies not only if you are seeking to renew a permission that has expired (see page 50), but also if your permission is different in detail from your new application. For example, an application for two houses on a site where two houses of different design had previously been approved could not justifiably (without special reason) be refused on the grounds that the principle of having two houses on the site was unacceptable; though it might, of course, be rejected on other grounds such as a poor or inappropriate design.

If a similar application to yours on the same site has previously been refused, that acts as a presumption that the new application will also be refused, unless other material factors (including local plan policies) have changed.

The size of an existing building on the site will influence the size allowable for a replacement building, although it does not follow automatically that you will be able to demolish one building and replace it by one of the same size.

A particularly relevant consideration, in planning terms, is whether the previous application was granted on appeal. A planning inspector's decision on an appeal is given more weight than a development control committee's initial decision, so this is a precedent which the local planning authority cannot ignore without very good reason.

ISSUES THAT ARE NOT PLANNING CONSIDERATIONS

There are strict legal limitations on the types of issue which local planning authorities can take into account when determining planning applications. The authority might have strong opinions on your application for a number of reasons, but be unable to take them into account because they are not strictly planning issues. Although all these issues are important from other perspectives, they should not be taken into account when your planning application is being considered. (However, you may well fall foul of other types of regulation if you ignore some of these issues.)

- The structural stability of new or existing buildings, including adjoining buildings. (However, this is an obvious example of where it pays to take care: planners may not prevent you from accidentally demolishing a neighbour's building, but your neighbour would certainly look for redress!)
- Private (as opposed to public) rights of way.
- The personal circumstances and identity of an applicant. This includes how long an individual applicant has lived in the area, or a business has operated in the area, and the applicant's motives. Planning applicants are not anonymous, but their reputation and contacts should carry no weight in a planning context. (There are some exceptions to this general rule, however: see pages 47 and 48.)
- The financial viability of the proposal. Planners are not concerned to assess your business plan, or find out whether you have funding in place. If you're proposing something that is unwise in business terms, that generally remains your concern, not theirs. (However, they will be concerned to avoid blighting a piece of land by approving a scheme which appears unlikely ever to be achieved.)

- The general effect of the proposal on the viability of other businesses. This is an issue which often arises in connection with commercial applications. Existing business owners cannot object to your proposed development on the grounds that you will provide competition which they would prefer not to face. The broad principle of national planning policy is that planning law is not to be used to restrain competition. However, planners can (and do) consider in broad terms the needs for commercial centres, and they might, for instance, reject a proposal for an out-of-town shopping precinct on the grounds that it would have a negative effect on a nearby town centre as a whole.

- Access across your site to maintain other property (although it is wise to be wary in case you infringe the legal rights of others in a non-planning sense).

- The safety of the materials you propose to use. (This is however controlled through building regulations: see Chapter 7.)

- The loss of views to existing residents or occupants. There are guidelines on 'rights of light' (ensuring that light falls on neighbouring windows), but your neighbours cannot object because your proposed development will block the view they currently enjoy. (However, see the note below about the Human Rights Act.)

- The effect of the development on the values of neighbouring properties.

- Future intentions of the applicant which are not covered by the planning application. You do not need to say that the application you have put forward is only Phase 1 of a four-stage expansion project, and indeed would probably be unwise to say so, unless you would face serious difficulties if later phases did not receive permission. However, some planning authorities may anticipate your intentions: they can require you to submit proposals at least in outline for an entire site, and resist giving piecemeal approvals.

- Disruption to neighbours and the general public during construction. (This does not mean, however, that you have *carte blanche* to disrupt the neighbourhood, as again, other types of regulation come into force here.)

HUMAN RIGHTS

It is not yet clear what effect Britain's signing up to European Human Rights legislation will have on the planning system, but most planners are agreed that it is likely to have some impact. The relevant sections are Articles 1 and 8 of the First Protocol. Both developers and those affected by developments have rights under the Human Rights Act, and it is likely that test cases over the next few years will help to define in what ways these rights apply in practice. At the time of writing, there is no significant case law on this issue, so it is not possible to give more guidance than an indication that this may prove to be a significant issue in future.

KEY POINTS

✔ *Applications for planning permission are considered within a framework of policy and law that stretches from the local to the international level.*

✔ *Planning permission applies to a site, not an applicant.*

✔ *Particularly important for local applicants are structure plans and local plans (sometimes combined as unitary plans).*

✔ *Planning permission does not give you a right to develop: other issues may stand in the way.*

✔ *Only certain issues can be considered by local planning authorities. Among those they do not consider are the viability of your proposal, and its effect on existing businesses.*

CHAPTER 3

Legal requirements

Objectives of the chapter:

- to explain when planning permission is needed
- to explain how to ascertain whether something is permissible without planning permission
- to explain the difference between outline and full planning permission
- to draw attention to some other types of permission that businesses may need to consider when expanding or relocating
- to introduce the issues of conservation areas, listed buildings and other areas and circumstances in which special permission applies
- to outline how pollution control relates to the planning process.

WHEN PLANNING PERMISSION IS NEEDED

As we have already explained, the planning system is concerned primarily with physical development that has an impact on the wider pattern of land use within the community, and with changes of use in the context of broad use classes (discussed in Chapter 2). Central to this is new development, but planning permission is not only needed for entirely new buildings. It is also needed:

- for most extensions and alterations affecting the external appearance of existing buildings
- for temporary structures of many kinds, though normally not for builders' huts
- for significant changes to the existing uses of land and buildings
- for large-scale tipping and excavation

- for many signs and display advertisements, both on buildings and stand-alone (though strictly, the requirement here is for advertisement consent rather than planning permission as such).

Permission is generally *not* required for:

- repairs and renovations which do not materially alter the building, although there are more restrictive rules for listed buildings (see page 33)
- changes of use within the same use class (provided they do not affect the external appearance of the premises, and with some specific exceptions).

However, because the legislation covering planning is complex, it is always as well to check with your local planning authority before assuming that planning permission is not necessary.

PERMITTED DEVELOPMENT

If the development you are planning is at all sizeable, the chances are you will need planning permission. However, the planning system would soon be choked up if every small change you made to your premises required permission – pathways resurfaced in different materials, for instance, or a different design of door when one needs replacing. The *de minimis* rule determines whether an alteration is sufficiently significant to require permission: if it is genuinely trivial, your local planning authority may well reassure you that permission is not necessary.

The *de minimis* rule applies to very, very small alterations, but some larger alterations are also allowed without specific permission, because they fall under the guidelines covering permitted development. These are legal guidelines (in the General Permitted Development Order 1995) which set out in detail what development is permissible without obtaining a specific permission (unlike the principle of *de minimis*, which is general and not fully defined in law). For example, permitted development applies to:

- factory and warehouse extensions up to a certain size (see the box opposite)
- temporary uses (such as fairs, fêtes and campsites) which apply for no more than 28 days each year in most cases (although some uses such as holding a market and motor vehicle racing are restricted to 14 days)
- some agricultural buildings
- domestic buildings, and in particular house extensions, new porches and garages and similar changes
- minor developments such as gates, fences, walls and hard standing for cars.

Although the General Permitted Development Order sets out broad classes of permitted development, there is scope for local planning authorities to reduce its scope. This is normally done using an 'Article 4 direction', a legal document issued by the local planning authority which specifies an area within which permitted development rights are removed or restricted, and the ways in which they are removed or restricted. Article 4 directions are often used to limit rights in conservation areas, where the design of buildings is considered to be particularly significant. In a terrace of houses of the same date and style, for example, the replacement of a flat window by a bay window, or building a porch, might be considered unacceptable, while in a more mixed and less architecturally sensitive suburban area it would be perfectly acceptable. Your local planning authority will again advise you on any particular rules which apply in your area.

EXTENSIONS TO FACTORIES AND WAREHOUSES

Factory or warehouse extensions do not require planning permission if they meet all the following criteria:

- The total floor space of the proposed extension(s) is less than 1,000 m² (although the limit is 500 m² in areas of special sensitivity such as National Parks, Areas of Outstanding Natural Beauty and conservation areas).
- The volume of the extension is less than 25 per cent of the volume of the original building (10 per cent in sensitive areas).
- The highest point of the extension is below the height of the original building.
- The proposed use of the extension is related to the current use of the existing building, or it is intended to house staff facilities.

- The extension does not materially affect the external appearance of the building (for example, it should be of a similar design).
- No part of the extension comes within 5 metres of the site boundary.
- Building the extension will not reduce the amount of space available for parking or for vehicles turning.

WORKING FROM HOME

A significant number of people have always worked from home, and this is becoming a particularly popular option in an era when IT and telecommunications mean that many information-related jobs can be carried on anywhere there is a computer and a phone point. Working from home represents a change of use, from residential to residential and part-business use (unless the use is very small-scale and domestic in character, in which case this is not regarded as a significant alteration), and in many cases it also requires alterations to your home in order to accommodate the business.

If you are making sizeable physical alterations, you are likely to need planning permission. Even if you are not, you may still need permission for the change of use. As with the exceptions discussed above, the main issue for planners in determining whether permission is needed is whether your change to business use makes a material difference to others. If you plan to write novels in your existing study, or to mind a neighbour's child, the effect on the land-use pattern of your neighbourhood will be minimal, and you will probably find there is no need to apply for permission. However, if you start up a car repair business in your garage and take on a couple of mechanics, or open up a nursery caring for a dozen small children, the planning authority will take a rather different attitude.

That your home is in a generally residential area will not necessarily prevent your obtaining planning permission for part-business use. Issues the planners will consider, in deciding both whether permission is needed and whether it should be granted, include:

- The number of visitors your business will generate.
- Whether any staff are to be employed (other than residents of the building).
- The amount of motor traffic the business will generate, and the ability of local roads to bear it.
- The need for parking that will be generated, and the ability to cope with it. (The local council will not be able to prevent commercial vehicles from being parked in unrestricted public roads, but they will be reluctant to approve uses which mean this will happen on a scale that affects others. They can prevent commercial vehicles from parking on domestic premises if this is out of keeping with the neighbourhood, or causes a nuisance.)
- The amount of noise the business will create.
- Whether the business can be considered as ancillary to domestic use (that is, if it is domestic in character, like bed-and-breakfast or childminding) or is quite separate in character.
- Whether the business is visible from the outside (for example, raw materials stored in your garden, a large sign on the wall) or is unobtrusive.
- The general tidiness of the site.

If you find planning permission is not necessary, this may not alter the fact that the building's use will be regarded as having changed. Generally, the regulations that apply to businesses will now apply to you. From a planning perspective, for example, you will not be able to take advantage of permitted development rights which apply to domestic uses only. You should be aware that business rates may be payable, and capital gains on selling your home will be taxed differently.

Whether it is strictly necessary or not, it would be wise to apply for permission if:

- you are planning to buy (or rent) a house with part-business use specifically in mind
- you will be investing heavily in your business, and would suffer were the use later to need, and fail to get, permission
- your neighbours are unhappy with your plans (or your existing activities) and you need the security of permission to counter their objections.

FLATS OVER SHOPS AND OFFICES

As was mentioned in Chapter 2, there are special exemptions which mean the upper storeys of office and shop buildings can normally be converted into residential accommodation (and back again) without planning permission, provided the external appearance is unchanged.

DEMOLITION

Planning permission is not generally required in order for you to be able to demolish an existing building, but conservation area or listed building consent may be necessary (see page 33) and you may be required to give prior notification to the local planning authority. However, the demolition process is controlled by the building control function, and you

should normally agree the demolition procedure with the building control department of your local planning authority unless one of the following conditions applies:

- The volume of the building is less than 50 m^3.
- The demolition is urgently necessary for health and safety reasons.
- The demolition is required under other legislation.
- The building is on land which has planning permission for redevelopment (of a kind which implies demolition of what already exists).

Unless it is in the curtilage (enclosed adjacent land) of a listed building, you do not need permission to demolish a gate, fence, wall or similar structure.

Demolition does not ensure that the building can be replaced. If you wish to replace it (even with an identical building), then you will need to apply for planning permission for the new build.

ADVERTISEMENTS

It is generally permissible to display a small advertisement or other sign on your premises without specific planning permission, but sizeable advertisements and signage do need permission. In general, planning permission is needed for displaying an advert which is larger than 0.3 m^2. In many cases permission is granted for five years only, though it is possible to apply for its renewal at the end of this period.

The rules are a little different for temporary notices relating to one-off events: usually no permission is needed unless they are larger than 0.6 m^2. (This does not mean that fly-posting on the property of others, or on public property, is permissible: see page 87.) There are also different rules for estate agents' boards.

More information on permission for advertisements is in Chapter 8.

EXISTING USES

As we explained earlier, the general presumption of the planning process is that long-existing buildings and uses are permitted to continue. However, this presumption is not intended to remove the need to apply for planning permission. If either you, or a previous owner or occupant, choose to ignore the planning legislation and make changes without permission, then you run the risk that enforcement action will be taken against you (see Chapter 9).

You may find it helpful to check with your local planning authority whether there are any permissions current on your site. The planning authority will have a record of the site's planning history, and will be able to advise you what planning applications have been granted or refused. (Remember: planning permission applies to the site, not the individual.) Planning permission also has a time limit. If development does not begin within the given time (usually five years), the permission lapses, so it may be that you will discover permissions for new developments that did not take place and are no longer authorised.

Although the planning authority can tell you about planning applications, they cannot automatically advise you whether a use or building that is currently on the site is legal, since that use or building may not need a specific per-

mission. It could predate the formal planning process, or it could post-date it and not have permission, but have been in existence for sufficiently long that it cannot now be challenged. If you want to reassure yourself that a use or building without formal planning permission is legal, you can apply to your local planning authority for a lawful development certificate.

Lawful development certificates

A lawful development certificate (or strictly, a certificate of lawful development) is a legal certification that a development that has taken place, or is to take place, is lawful and either has or does not need planning permission. It is rather trickier to obtain than planning permission, so it is less well used. You might choose to apply for it when:

- you think planning permission is not required, but you suspect that if you did apply for it, it would be refused
- you think planning permission is not required, but you suspect that if you did apply for it, the council would only grant it subject to unacceptable conditions (for example, severe restriction on opening hours)
- you think the council is likely to take enforcement action against a development or use which is in existence, and you want to pre-empt them by proving the development is legal.

WHEN PLANNING PERMISSION IS NOT ENOUGH

One theme we have emphasised in this book is that planning permission does not give you a right to carry out a development; it only facilitates it. These are some of the issues which may make it difficult to proceed with a development even if it obtains planning permission.

31

Ownership and occupation of a site

You do not need to be the owner of a site to apply for planning permission on that site, but you do need to advise the owner (see Chapter 4). However, obtaining planning permission is not a shortcut to obtaining the site to which it applies. If the site is not yours, then you cannot compel the owner to sell it to you or to develop it in accordance with the planning permission.

If you have existing tenants with valid leases, or any other legal right to remain in occupation, then obtaining planning permission will not entitle you to invalidate their leases and develop your property. It is up to you to ensure that the way is clear for development.

Covenants, easements and conditions in leases

A covenant on your freehold property, or a clause in your lease, may restrict what you can do with the land or property. For example, your lease may specify that your premises are to be used only for specific purposes, or cannot be used for other specific purposes. Planning permission cannot remove or alter a covenant, and it does not affect the terms of your lease, so you will still be unable to do anything that is restricted in this way.

An easement is a statutory right of others which limits what you can do with your own land. For example, other people may have the right to have their buildings supported by your land, or to light and air that travels across your land. They will have access to recourse against you if you do not maintain the easement.

Rights of way

Public rights of way are mostly now covered by statute law, particularly the Highways Act 1980. A grant of planning permission does not give you permission to interfere with, move or obstruct a public right of way. A path cannot legally be diverted or closed unless the council has made an order to divert or close it, a process which involves advertisement and gives the public and other interested parties an opportunity to object. (In the event of objections, an independent inspector will resolve the issue on behalf of the Secretary of State.) When you are likely to need an order, you should apply for it before you start the development.

THE PRESERVATION OF OUR HERITAGE

As we have already discussed, one of the aims of the land-use planning system is to ensure that what is of value in both the built and the natural environment is preserved, conserved and where possible enhanced. Many policies have been adopted, and regulations enacted, to this end. In large part, the planning system is the medium for enforcing these. In some cases additional permissions are required as well as normal planning permission, but in general local planning authorities will not give planning permission unless other relevant permissions are in place.

Vegetation and wildlife

If the site in question harbours existing rare plant species, or is a wildlife habitat, then the law may prevent you from developing it in ways which would harm the plants or wildlife, especially if it is designated as a SSI, SAC or Ramsar site. The EC Habitats Directive 1992 (properly, the Directive on the Conservation of Natural Habitats and of Wild Flora and Fauna) is a key piece of legislation in this area. Generally speaking, the conservation of wildlife is integrated with the planning system, so you will not receive planning permission for a development that is unacceptably damaging to the ecosystem, but there are some specific laws which operate separately.

Specific legislation protects the roosts of bats, and it is a criminal offence to disturb these.

Trees covered by tree preservation orders, and all trees in conservation areas, cannot be felled or pruned without specific permission being given. Again, planners should alert you if this affects your proposal. If planning permission has been granted and it is necessary to fell the trees in order to implement it, then this counts as permission to do so. (See also page 81.)

Listed buildings

A listed building is a building of special architectural or historical interest which has been included in a list compiled by the Secretary of State for Transport, Local Government and the Regions. Many buildings were listed at the introduction of the system in the mid-twentieth century, but the list continues to be revised, and many more buildings have been added since. Listing a building is normally a fairly slow process, but if a building is perceived to be under threat of demolition or substantial alteration, it can be rapidly 'spot listed' to protect it.

Buildings are designated by three grades. Grade I buildings are of national interest, and this category is applied largely to public buildings, museums, major historic country houses and the like. Grades II* and II apply to buildings that are of sufficient merit or interest to deserve preservation, but that are not of such national significance. Among the buildings in these categories are many buildings which today house businesses: not just shops and offices in old buildings in historic town and city centres, but factories, office blocks and the like from all periods up to and including modern times. A building need not be old to be listed. Serious efforts have been made in recent years to ensure that a representative proportion of well-designed buildings from all decades of the twentieth century are preserved for future generations.

There are limitations on alterations to, demolition of, and construction on the sites (including the curtilage) of listed buildings which are much more severe than those on unlisted buildings. If your proposal involves a listed building, it is necessary to obtain listed building consent to any changes as well as planning permission (see page 77).

Below the categories of nationally listed buildings is a separate category of buildings of 'local interest'. These are listed by local planning authorities, rather than by the Secretary of State, and once they have been listed, the local planning authority is required to pay special regard when considering proposals affecting them. Buildings on the 'local list' do not need listed building consent, but they cannot be demolished without consent if they are in a conservation area (see below).

Conservation areas

Conservation areas are also defined by local planning authorities, via a programme of public consultation. The definitions are regularly reviewed, and new areas defined as the local planning authorities find appropriate.

A conservation area is a neighbourhood of specific character which is considered worthy of preservation. As with listed buildings, it need not be picturesque or entirely historic in nature; a well-preserved suburban estate can be designated as a conservation area, and many town and city centres have been designated in whole or in part.

The legislation governing conservation areas provides a greater than normal degree of protection against the demolition of buildings and felling of trees. Tighter than normal design guidelines usually apply in conservation areas (including guidelines on allowable materials), as do restrictions in the general rights of developers to carry out small developments without planning permission (see Chapter 4).

Green belts, National Parks, Areas of Outstanding Natural Beauty and other protected land

These designations – which also include SSIs, SACs and Ramsar sites – generally apply to relatively undeveloped areas in which the natural, rather than the built, landscape is the subject of conservation. There is a presumption against development in most of these areas, and in some cases it is virtually certain that development will not be permitted.

Development is not prevented in National Parks, which cover sizeable areas of land, but it is subject to particular control, and the National Park authorities play a formal role in the planning process.

Green belts cover about 12 per cent of the area of England. (There are currently none in Wales.) They are designated:

- to stop urban sprawl, when large towns and cities coalesce with each other
- to control the expansion of larger settlements so they maintain a coherent form, and to protect their setting
- to help to safeguard the countryside from encroachment under development pressure
- to encourage urban regeneration, by forcing developers to look instead at 'brownfield' sites.

Sometimes there are existing settlements within the green belt, but there is still a presumption that expansion and infilling (that is, development on vacant sites within the settlement boundary) will not be allowed. However, it is normally acceptable for derelict buildings within green belts to be returned to productive uses.

SIMPLIFIED PLANNING ZONES

As well as areas where development is restricted or prevented, there are areas where development is particularly encouraged. In simplified planning zones, which were introduced in 1986, the usual controls on development are relaxed (in specified ways) so as to encourage development or redevelopment. Designation allows the local planning authority to grant a general planning permission for the area, and developers can then carry out development within the scope of the general planning permission without the need to apply for further planning permission.

These zones include action areas, designated in local plans as areas that the local planning authority has selected for comprehensive improvement or development over a ten-year period. The local plan will outline the type of improvement or development that is being looked for.

Enterprise zones, which are specifically employment-oriented areas for development, also have specific planning rules. The Secretary of State has the power to invite a local authority to prepare a scheme for an enterprise zone. When adopted, it provides for specified categories of development to automatically have planning permission.

OTHER TYPES OF PERMISSION

As well as the factors discussed above, you need to be aware of the broad spread of legislation and control that may affect you, both while your development is in progress, and once it is completed and your activities are in operation.

While building is in progress

When you carry out construction work, it must be done in a lawful way and with proper respect for the rights of the public and neighbours. Health and safety and environmental health regulations control not only the general process of operating on site, but also aspects such as the hours within which building work can take place.

Many of the detailed aspects of building design and construction are overseen by the building control system. It is, of course, essential that you comply with building regulations and obtain all the necessary certificates (see Chapter 7).

When you begin to operate

Planning permission does not automatically give you permission to extract water from the public supply, to dispose of waste, or to operate processes that may cause pollution. All of these activities are carefully regulated, and you need to be aware of the regulations as they affect your business. Detailed discussion of them is beyond the scope of this book.

The grant of planning permission for a restaurant, club, pub or other premises selling alcohol or providing entertainment does not automatically grant the necessary licences to do these things. Alcohol licences are currently granted by magistrates (though this system is under review, and could change in future), and take into account factors which are not considered in the planning process, including the character of the individual applicant, as well as factors which overlap with the planning process, such as the noise generated by the establishment.

Local authorities currently administer public entertainment licences, which are required for public dancing, or any music and singing with more than two performers, and late night refreshment house licences, which are required for any house, room, shop or building kept open for public refreshment and entertainment between 10 pm and 5 am. Generally these licences are subject to annual renewal. (These are not needed for takeaways.)

TYPES OF PLANNING PERMISSION

There are a number of different types of planning permission of which you should be aware. (The details of how to make applications are covered in Chapter 4.)

Outline planning permission

Outline planning permission (OPP) is intended to establish in principle whether a new building will be permitted. It is not normal to apply for OPP for extensions or alterations, and not possible to make outline applications for changes of use.

OPP is useful when you want to:

- get agreement to the principle of your development without going to the expense of drawing up a detailed proposal
- sell a site with permission for development, but leave the details to the purchaser
- establish the general scale and size of buildings that will be permitted, to provide a guideline when firming up the development.

Local planning authorities are not always obliged to consider applications for OPP: for environmentally sensitive sites, they have the right to insist on a full application instead.

Once OPP has been granted, the applicant has three years within which to make a 'reserved matters' application, which provides the detail and (when approved) transforms the OPP into full planning permission. It is possible to make any number of different reserved matters applications, although only one can be combined with the OPP to make a full permission.

Full planning permission

This provides as much detail as is necessary to the local planning authority, and when granted, gives the applicant permission to proceed with the development, subject, of course, to all the provisos we noted above.

Advertisement consent

The Control of Advertisement Regulations 1992 give 'deemed consent' to many smaller adverts displayed outdoors – on the outside of buildings, on hoardings and so on – such as nameplates for businesses and short-term posters for local events. To display other types of outdoor advertisement (including adverts on parts of your building not normally used for that purpose) you need to apply for *advertisement consent* (a process broadly similar to a standard planning application).

MULTIPLE PERMISSIONS FOR THE SAME SITE

If you have planning permission for one development, that does not prevent you from making an application for another development on the same site. Receiving permission for the second development does not normally invalidate the existing permission; while both permissions remain current, you can decide which one you will choose to implement. Often you can only implement one of the permissions because they are mutually exclusive and make different proposals for the same land. However, sometimes multiple applications are made that are not mutually exclusive: for example, there may be one application for a building to be erected at the west end of a site, and another application for a building to be erected at the east end. If the local planning authority would be prepared to see either, but not both, developments take place, they might insist on a revocation of the first planning permission before the second was granted.

CONTROL OF POLLUTION AND THE PLANNING PROCESS

The general guidance covering the land-use planning system is that it is not intended to duplicate the statutory responsibilities of other bodies. So planners do not pre-empt the role of magistrates (at present although this is likely to change) in deciding the suitability of applicants for alcohol licences, and similarly, they do not pre-empt the roles of the Environment Agency, of local authorities and of other bodies in controlling potentially polluting processes.

This is not the place for a full description of pollution control. The core piece of legislation in this field is the Environment Protection Act 1990. Businesses subject to its legislation cannot operate without pollution control consents, licences or authorisations where they are required. The pollution control system generally operates in accordance with the precautionary principle (that scientific evidence does not need to be conclusive for it to be advisable to anticipate and try to prevent risks to the environment), and is moving towards the principle of integrated pollution prevention and control, a system which takes account of all sources of pollution and all the natural elements (earth, water, air) in which pollution can occur.

Where land-use planning does have a legitimate role is in determining in outline where potentially polluting activities should be located. Structure plans and local plans are expected to make provision for dirty and 'bad neighbour' uses, and of course, to do so taking account of the wider pattern of uses into which these have to fit. The potential for pollution to affect the use of the land can also be a material consideration in deciding whether to grant planning permission (or to take enforcement action against an existing unauthorised use of land), so it is legitimate for a local planning authority to refuse planning permission where they feel that potential pollution could have an impact on the development and use of land (including neighbouring land) to an extent that is unacceptable on planning grounds. Of course, the refusal of planning permission to a development that has pollution control authorisations does not invalidate those authorisations, any more than the refusal of the authorisations invalidates an existing planning permission.

In the past, there were separate planning regulations for 'bad neighbour' uses, but this is not the case today; these are considered via the normal planning process.

The final role of the planning system in a pollution context is to control other development that is close to actual, or potential, sources of pollution. For example, a planning authority would be wary of granting permission for housing in close proximity to a chemical factory or landfill site.

Any proposal where risk of pollution is significant needs to be considered with particular care, and for this reason, local planning authorities will not normally accept applications for outline planning permission in these cases.

ONE–STOP SHOPS

It will be clear that although efforts are made in some directions to co-ordinate the overall system of approval and regulation, the result is still a minefield for the unwary applicant. It is all right knowing that you can have planning permission without permission to operate your industrial processes in the finished building, but needless to say, no applicant wants that to happen.

The government is working towards developing a more integrated system, in which applicants only have to apply to one source in order to get all the different approvals they require. As a first step, some pilot projects have been set up to provide 'one-stop shops' for applicants. The local planning authority usually acts as the 'one-stop', passing on applications as appropriate, and obtaining advice from specialist bodies such as water companies, English Heritage and the Environment Agency.

Some of the features of the pilot projects are:

- Co-ordinated pre-application discussions, so that applicants can have a clear picture of what everyone involved requires before they proceed too far.
- A designated case officer who acts as the single point of contact.
- Co-ordinated site visits, so businesses are not disrupted by a stream of representatives from different bodies arriving to inspect the premises at different times.

As yet, this initiative is in its early stages, but it is certainly welcomed by most applicants, and it is to be hoped that it will be developed and will eventually become the norm.

KEY POINTS

✔ *Planning permission is needed generally for new build, for significant extensions and alterations, and for various other land-use changes. It is not needed for repairs and renovations.*

✔ *Many small alterations can be handled without planning permission, but it is always as well to check.*

✔ *You need not own a site to apply for planning permission, but planning permission does not give you the right to override the rights of owners, tenants or other interested parties.*

✔ *The building process is not controlled through the planning system, but primarily via the building control system.*

✔ *Other permissions you may need include alcohol and public entertainment licences and pollution control authorisations.*

✔ *Special restrictions apply to listed buildings, in conservation areas, in green belts, and in areas of ecological importance.*

✔ *It can be useful to apply for outline planning permission, particularly when you have no immediate plans to start the development.*

✔ *One-stop shops are being piloted as a way of streamlining the consent process.*

Making a planning application

This chapter deals with the practical business of making a planning application. Once you have read it you should understand:

- who to make your application to
- what expert help is available
- how to research your proposal
- how to get your proposal drawn up
- about expiry and renewal of planning permission
- how to make a 'reserved matters' application.

THE FRAMEWORK FOR GRANTING PLANNING PERMISSION

The core information that follows applies primarily to England. The rules are slightly different in Scotland and Wales, and substantially different in Northern Ireland (see page 40).

The development control process is handled by local planning authorities (LPAs) who can be either 'district' or 'county' in level. Before local government reorganisation in the 1990s, these were in most cases literally district and county councils, but now a wider range of local government bodies are involved.

District matters

District-level planning authorities comprise:

- metropolitan and non-metropolitan district councils
- unitary authorities (in this capacity)
- London boroughs
- National Park authorities.

They deal with all planning applications except for a limited number involving 'county matters', which are outlined below.

FINDING YOUR LOCAL PLANNING AUTHORITY

Normally, your local planning authority will be the local government body that issues your council tax bill. Contact details should be available in your local phone book, and virtually all councils now have websites (simply type in the name of your town or district to a search engine and see what comes up). If you're not certain which local authority area your site is located in, give any nearby local authority a call and they will advise you.

Councils are organised in various ways, and sometimes there will not be a 'planning department' as such, but the switchboard should be able to advise you which department deals with planning applications. Some local planning authorities divide their area into geographical regions: make a note of the region into which your site falls, and of the contact person to whom you are referred.

SOME FACTS AND FIGURES

- There are 362 district-level planning authorities in England.
- Over 95% of planning applications are decided by local planning authorities.
- In the last quarter of 2000, district-level planning authorities received 122,000 applications for planning permission and related consents. There were increases in the number received in Yorkshire, the Humber and the South West (up 5 per cent) and East Midlands (up 4 per cent) and a decrease in London (down 2 per cent).
- In the last quarter of 2000, 87 per cent of applications were granted (a number that remains relatively stable from year to year).

County matters

'County matters' are mostly concerned with waste disposal (which accounts for about 51 per cent of county-level planning applications) and minerals extraction (which accounts for about 31 per cent). County councils also generally handle applications for their own developments. Since county applications are very much a minority, unless you are certain that your application concerns a county matter you should make your application in the first place to your district authority.

The county-level authorities in England are:

- county councils (157, handling 82 per cent of applications)
- metropolitan districts (handling 10 per cent of applications)
- unitary authorities (handling 7 per cent)
- London boroughs.

COUNTY-LEVEL PLANNING APPLICATIONS

- There are about 2,000 applications for 'county matters' planning permission each year.
- About 90 per cent of these applications are granted.
- Decisions are slower than for district matters: only about 50 per cent are made within 17 weeks.

NORTHERN IRELAND

As we mentioned earlier, the system for determining applications is different (and rather less democratic) in Northern Ireland. The Department of the Environment for Northern Ireland (DoENI) acts as a unitary planning authority, regulating development and use of land. Appeals against their decisions are heard by a separate Planning Appeals Commission

The Environment and Heritage Service, a separate agency within the DoENI, provides specialist advice on issues concerned with the historic environment. Most of the planning law is similar to that in England, but there are a few significant differences: for example, trees in conservation areas are automatically protected from felling in England, but in Northern Ireland they are not protected unless they are covered by a tree preservation order.

THE PROCESS FOR MAKING A PLANNING APPLICATION

Some planning applications are for very major new developments costing millions of pounds; others are for small alterations costing perhaps only a few hundred. Obviously the time and effort that needs to be put into the applications will not be the same in each case, but the general process is the same. This is the outline process. (All these steps are discussed in more detail later in the chapter.)

- The applicant checks what kinds of permission are needed and to whom application should be made.
- (Optionally, but in many cases) the applicant contacts the local planning authority informally and discusses the application in outline. (Of course, at this stage the applicant will also research and start the process of applying for other necessary types of permit or licence.)
- The applicant decides who will prepare the application. It may be simple enough for you or your staff to handle, but in many cases you will need expert input.
- The applicant researches the issues and draws up a brief for any experts involved.
- The applicant and/or experts acting as the applicant's agents draw up plans and proposals.

- The applicant (or his/her agent) makes a formal application for planning permission.
- The local planning authority checks that the application is complete and (of course, after the fee has been paid) logs it in a register.
- The local planning authority issues notice of the application to statutory and other consultees, and puts a copy on deposit for the public to consult.
- Consultees review the application and give their feedback if they wish.
- The general public have an opportunity to review the application and submit their comments.
- A planning officer (a member of the local planning authority staff) inspects the site, considers the results of the consultation process, and decides whether the application needs to go before a development control (DC) committee, or can be handled by the local planning authority staff under delegated powers.
- Assuming the application is not handled under delegated powers (see below) the planning officer writes a report for the development control committee.
- The development control committee reviews the application and makes a decision (or in some cases, makes a provisional decision and delegates final negotiations to the planning officer, or decides on a site visit before making a decision).
- The planning officer sends a decision notice to the applicant and records the decision in the local planning authority's records.

GETTING EXPERT HELP

Unless your application is very minor, or you have experts in-house, you will almost certainly need help in drawing up your application. Your local planning authority staff will give you a degree of guidance, but it is not their job to prepare your application for you. Among the sources of possible help are:

Architects They are of course experts in building design, but they may not be as expert in wider land-use issues such as transport implications. However, architects suited to your proposal should be able to recommend other experts to you as necessary. Of course, architects do not come cheap, but they are well qualified to do a thorough job for you, and can in most cases be thoroughly recommended as a source of assistance.

Architectural technicians These are not fully qualified architects, and as a result they tend to come a little cheaper. Many architectural technicians do a great deal of work drawing up plans and preparing planning applications.

Surveyors These, too, are professionals in aspects of the development process, and for suitable projects prove excellent sources of advice, but they may not be expert in all land-use issues.

Planning consultants These are professionals with town-planning rather than architectural qualifications. Many of them are former local planning authority staff, so they have an in-depth knowledge of how the planning system works in practice. A planning consultant will not design your building, but he or she will be able to give you good advice on the wider issues that affect your planning application. If your application is large or complex, you may find that you need to retain a planning consultant as well as an architect. Some planning consultants specialise in particular land-use aspects such as transport or ecological issues. The Royal Town Planning Institute (RTPI) maintains a register of planning consultants who operate in each geographical area.

Planning Aid This is a free advice service for those who cannot afford to retain specialist advisers (see below).

Builders and 'design and build' firms If your development is simple and straightforward, you may not feel able to justify the expense of employing a qualified architect. Most large building firms have considerable experience of the planning process, and many will offer you advice and assistance. 'Design and build' firms which offer streamlined design services in conjunction with construction services, are in a relatively good position to provide broad planning advice. Some will have qualified architects or planners on board, but it is as well to check what qualifications any adviser of this nature actually possesses. 'Design and build' firms tend to offer tried and tested designs. If you (or your planning authority) want something more individual, an architect may be preferable. Smaller local builders tend to have less wide experience and knowledge: they may be able to help you draw up a simple plan, but it would be unwise to rely too much on their expertise.

Solicitors Many small business people turn to solicitors because they see planning as a legal process of the kind which would be familiar to solicitors (and of course, because solicitors are professionals whom they already know). However, very few solicitors have any in-depth expertise in this field, and generally you would be better advised to ensure that your adviser has particular experience in the planning area.

Why you need expert advice

Almost all advice costs, but a good expert should more than save you the cost of his or her fee. The right expert or experts:

- Will help to ensure that your development is fitted for its purpose, designed with energy and operating efficiency in mind, attractive in appearance, and generally in conformance with sustainable development principles.

- Will understand wider land-use issues and be able to point you towards aspects to which you need to give particular consideration.

- Will be familiar with planning policies from the local to the national (and international) level, and will help to ensure that your application conforms to them.

- Will know how to offset positive and less welcome aspects of your proposal so that the balance overall tips in your favour.

- Will know how to phrase the application so as to emphasise positive points and avoid including information which might jeopardise its chances.

- Will be familiar with the local planning authority's procedures, their general approach, their priorities and preferences, and quite possibly with the staff who handle your application and the councillors who may decide on it. All of this helps you to tailor your application so as to improve its chances of success.

Planning Aid

'Planning Aid' is a free service provided by planning professionals. It is intended to provide general advice to individuals, community groups and other voluntary groups who cannot afford to pay for private consultants. It is administered by the RTPI, whose Corporate Members participate in it on a voluntary basis, providing advice on applications in areas other than their own (if they work for local planning authorities). Those involved:

- explain how the system works
- help applicants to present their own proposals
- help individuals and groups to comment on proposals which affect them or their community
- provide advice on development plans, and help individuals and groups to participate in the consultation process (see Chapter 10).

CONSULTATIONS

You are not obliged to speak to anyone at your local planning authority before submitting your application, or while it is being considered, but often it is wise to do so, particularly if your proposal is sizeable, or is likely to be controversial for any reason. Two types of individual deal with your planning application: elected members, and officers of the council. You can contact either at any stage in the process.

Planning officers

Planning officers are members of staff of the local planning authority. As planning professionals, it is their job to see your application through the process, and they do of course have professional qualifications and all the necessary knowledge to do so. There is no charge for consulting them (beyond the scale charge for your application), but you should of course bear in mind that they have limited time, and plenty of calls on the time they have.

HOW TO CONSULT A PLANNING OFFICER

- A phone call is often the best first step. If this indicates that a meeting would be useful, you can go on to arrange one.

- If you have a straightforward factual query, or need to obtain a form, e-mail or fax may be acceptable alternatives.

- Many development control departments will accept drop-in callers, but if you want to discuss an application in detail it is better to make an appointment with the appropriate officer.

- You can suggest a site visit at an early stage, or the officer may suggest it to you.

- Prepare well for your meeting. Bring along a plan of the site, and/or photographs of the existing buildings, and all the information you can muster on your proposals.

- Have it clear in your mind what you want to do. It is not the job of the planning officer to draw up your proposal, only to comment on it.

Reasons for consulting with planning officers

- You can make sure that the local planning authority has all relevant information, whether or not it is required on the application form.

- The planning officer will have a good background in planning regulations, and will be able to advise you if any aspects of your proposal are likely to be unacceptable.

- The planning officer will be familiar with the local plan and structure plan, so can set your application in a wider policy framework; and, for example, advise what uses are likely to be acceptable on the site you have in mind, or point you to other possible sites which might be more appropriate for your use.

- The planning officer can advise you about the planning history of the site, and point you to any other useful information (for example, a planning brief may have been prepared for the site, or there may be supplementary design guidance for the area).

- If the application is a simple one, and the officer indicates it is likely to be acceptable with no difficulty, you can minimise the amount of work you (or your agents) put into it.

- If the application does raise problems, the officer can steer you towards amending it to make it more acceptable.

- On some applications, a planning officer (not necessarily the one with whom you have consulted) will make the decision on the application.

- On all other applications, the planning officer will be responsible for recommending acceptance or refusal to the development control committee.

- If conditions are likely to be placed on the application, you can negotiate directly with the officer to help ensure they are acceptable to you.

Points to be wary of when consulting with planning officers

- Listen carefully to the feedback you receive. If you are told an application is likely to be unacceptable, then consider carefully how you might revise it to make it more acceptable.

- Be cautious in deciding what information you want to give the officer. For example, if this application is for phase one of a development programme, and you are not sure that later phases will be acceptable, it may not be to your benefit to sketch out the whole programme at this stage.

- Bear in mind that the officer's job is to give impartial advice to the development control committee, not to make policy decisions.
- Remember that the planning officer cannot take into account issues that are not considered relevant in planning terms, such as your personal circumstances.
- Do not expect the officer to draw up your proposal for you, or to draft alterations to it. This is a job for you and your paid advisers.
- Take up no more time than is necessary. Planning officers cannot spend unlimited time discussing straightforward applications, they are simply too busy.
- And, of course, avoid offering anything that could be construed as bribery or coercion.

Members

Members (that is, local councillors, or appointees on bodies such as National Park authorities) are not normally qualified land-use planners. Their role is to ensure that decisions are taken democratically and that the public's voice is heard. That said, some members sit on development control committees for many years, all are now expected to receive training, and many attend professional conferences and acquire a considerable amount of expertise. A good and experienced committee member will not only know the area intimately; he or she will also have a reasonable grasp of planning law and the planning process.

You can contact:

- any or all of the councillors who represent your local ward
- the chair or vice chair of the development control committee that will be considering your application

- if you feel it necessary, all members of the development control committee.

Councillors are bound by a strict code of conduct, and this will help to determine how they respond to your approach (see below).

HOW TO CONTACT A COUNCIL MEMBER

- All local authorities provide information on request on their elected members, including the political party they represent and their contact details. Phone, or check the council website.
- You can write to the councillor at the council offices, and the letter will be forwarded. It is not advisable to phone a councillor at the council offices, except by pre-arrangement: councillors are not council employees and do not keep office hours. Many have separate jobs, and have only limited time to give to their council activities.
- You can phone the councillor at their contact number, or e-mail or fax them in many cases.
- Bear in mind that councillors are busy people, and that their service is voluntary: they are paid an expense allowance but not normally a salary. If you want purely factual information, or a form to complete, ask the council staff, not the members. Keep letters and phone calls short, and do not request face-to-face meetings unless, and until, they are really necessary.
- If you feel it would be helpful for members to view your site, or you want to show them plans you cannot reasonably copy, then be prepared to negotiate arrangements to meet their needs. It is no use inviting councillors with full-time jobs to turn up at your site at your chosen time: they'll only come if they agree that it is necessary, and if the meeting is at a time they have confirmed with you.

(continued overleaf)

HOW TO CONTACT A COUNCIL MEMBER *(continued)*

- Party politics should play little part in development control, but if you are a member or supporter of a political party, you can of course choose to talk to a councillor who represents that party. If your party is not represented in the ward where your site is located, you may find that the party has arrangements for councillors representing other wards to give advice. If it isn't represented on the council at all, you may find aspiring candidates willing to lobby or advise you.

- If you are looking for a councillor to put your case for you, it is often better to ask one who is not a member of the development control committee, since a member may be disqualified from voting on the application if he or she becomes overly involved with you and your application.

- Your MP is usually not the right person to contact, unless your development is of major significance to your area, and/or it runs into difficulties which you have been unable to resolve at a lower level.

Reasons for consulting with members

- The members of the development control committee are the ones who, in many but not all cases, actually make the decision on your application (see below).

- Members are responsible for the local planning authority's individual policy decisions, including policy input to local and structure plans (although, of course, they are only free to make decisions within limits defined by planning law and by the policy framework that has been set down at higher levels).

- Members tend to take a broad viewpoint, rather than a narrow land-use viewpoint. They will be guided by officers in making decisions that are sustainable on planning grounds, but they may weigh economic issues (such as potential new jobs, or the urgent need to expand your premises in order to modernise the business) more heavily than do officers. You can also mention to them issues that are not strictly planning issues – such as your personal circumstances – in the knowledge that although they cannot use these as criteria in determining their application, they may still affect their attitude towards it.

- Some members (particularly the more senior and/or experienced) have a wide range of knowledge and contacts that could be useful to you in a more general sense in pursuing your development.

Points to be wary of when consulting with members

- Remember that members are busy people with only limited time to spare. They should always be prepared to meet with you to discuss policy issues, but it is not their job to act as development control staff. If you take up their time disproportionately, or ask them to run errands for you, you may inadvertently make them hostile.

- Do not take it for granted that the members you speak to will support your application. They have to balance your wants and needs with those of the wider community they represent. Your application may be unacceptable on policy or legal grounds which members are not free to override. Remember too that the decision will be taken on planning grounds alone: explaining about your personal or business circumstances may make members well disposed to the application, but it will not and cannot ensure that the application gets approved.

- Do not ask a development control committee member whether he or she will support you: he or she should not decide on the application until it has been discussed at the committee meeting.

- Avoid threats and bullying tactics. A good member will not be swayed by threats to withdraw support from them in future, or to move the business from the area. Repeat the threats to your local newspaper, and you will most likely make an enemy.

- It is essential to bear in mind the distinction between lobbying (which is perfectly acceptable) and bribery (which is illegal). Offering a cup of tea is fine; offering a disproportionately lavish meal is not, and offering money or gifts is definitely out.

- Members are governed by rules which oblige them to make public any personal interest they have in an application, and if the interest is substantial (for example, they are shareholders in a company involved) then they can take no part in determining the application. Their code of conduct requires them to make it public if they have discussed the application with you before the meeting. If you invite members to visit your application site, you may find that they prefer to come as a group rather than individually, and/or accompanied by officers, to ensure that everything is seen to be above board.

CONDITIONS AND PLANNING OBLIGATIONS

This chapter is primarily about making your application, rather than about the way it proceeds from that point on (which is covered in the next chapter). Conditions attached to the planning approval often become a point of issue at a later stage, but sometimes they are worth negotiating right from the start.

Planning conditions

A condition is a clause attached to a planning approval which limits it in some way, and/or when permission would not have been granted without them. They cover issues such as:

- Limitation on the hours of operation of a business (that is, preventing late night or weekend operation of a takeaway food shop or a leisure facility) which might prove disruptive to neighbours.

- Requirements to submit and have agreed additional details, for example, on the design of the building, materials to be used, or the design of road access points, before construction can proceed.

- Requirements for soundproofing, or the checking of noise levels.

- Requirements for landscaping proposals to be agreed before work can proceed.

- The phasing of a large development.

- Time limits for development to commence.

- Requirements for land to be restored after disruption (for example, after mineral excavation).

- Variations in the conventional timescale for implementation of the approval.

- Personal permissions: allowing one named person to carry out the development. The presumption is against these, but this condition is put on approval in some cases. These conditions are most often attached to applications for a change of use, but they can also be attached to applications for physical development in some circumstances. (For example, alterations to a listed building to accommodate someone with a severe physical handicap might be allowed on the condition that the alterations were removed should the person leave the building.)

- Temporary permissions: for example, a short-term use of land, or permission for a temporary prefabricated building.

The conditions are added by the planning staff or development control committee to your application: it is not usual for the applicant to specify them. However, early discussions can often indicate where conditions are likely to be attached, and these may give you an opportunity to negotiate and to indicate where they may be acceptable to you, or where they would certainly not be acceptable. For example, to an applicant with premises in a suburban side street, a limitation on the opening hours of a takeaway to 11 pm might be perfectly acceptable; a city centre applicant looking to pick up trade from those leaving nightclubs might find it had a major and unacceptable effect on the business.

Sometimes the suggestion is made that it should be a condition of the application that occupation of the premises is restricted to the applicant only, or to a local firm only. (This can be suggested by applicants, for example, if they feel there is a pressing reason for their own firm to expand, but they accept that the proposed expansion is strictly contrary to planning policy.) Such conditions are rarely used: they are regarded as undesirable in principle because they would restrict competition. However, if you feel that your business has an exceptional need for the development you propose, it is open to you to suggest this. The condition will only be put on the application if the alternative is refusal. This option is generally only used for larger applications, and the condition often includes a time limit of less than ten years, so this could be agreed if you were, for example, envisaging a move to larger premises in a few years' time.

Temporary permission is sometimes granted when the application is for a change of use and it is arguable whether this is going to prove acceptable. For example, an application for a change from shop premises to a takeaway Indian restaurant might be given temporary permission if neighbours had expressed concern that the restaurant would generate traffic, rubbish and smells, but the applicants had protested that all these issues had been considered and solutions found. Similarly, use of a forecourt or wide pavement outside a pub or restaurant as an eating area might be approved on a temporary basis. The legal guidelines for local planning authorities is that they must be reasonable in setting the temporary period of time, which should not be too short to be practicable: that is, it will often be measured in years rather than months. As applicant, you might find this type of permission an acceptable compromise; equally, if your development involved you in considerable expense, you might feel it was unacceptable.

Planning obligations

Section 106 of the Town and Country Planning Act 1990 gave local planning authorities the right to negotiate 'planning obligations' or 'planning agreements' with developers in some circumstances. (These are also known as 'Section 106 agreements'.) Planning obligations are usually entered into when it is not practicable for some reason to place a condition on a planning approval. Sometimes this is because they are concerned mainly with things that a developer agrees to do *beyond* the boundary of the application site. Often they deal with transport issues: the widening of a road, or provision of a road junction with traffic lights to give easy access to a development site. They may concern other parts of the infrastructure such as the drainage system. Sometimes they concern wider land-use issues: for example, the developer of part of a housing estate might agree to provide a playground elsewhere on the estate, or some other community facility. (In these cases, the developer might make a 'commuted payment', that is, pay a cash sum towards the provision.)

As with conditions, planning obligations are generally agreed only when the application would not be acceptable without them. For example, the development might have inadequate road access and would not be acceptable without the road improvements; or it might be in a location that was inaccessible by public transport, which made it unacceptable in policy terms. The additional proposed housing might conflict with local guidelines on the provision of open space or play equipment, and so on. When local planning authorities routinely expect those concerned with specific types of development to enter into planning obligations, they are expected to make this policy clear in the local plan.

Planning obligations are usually discussed at an early stage in the process of the application, though they will not be agreed formally until planning permission is given. More typically they are attached to large developments; it would not be usual for a small shopkeeper, say, to enter into a planning obligation.

The general government guideline on planning obligations it that they should be directly related to the proposed development, and should be proportional to it in scale. There is sometimes a narrow line between requiring improvements to be made in order to facilitate the development, and wanting improvements to be made, or facilities provided, that the local authority cannot otherwise afford. It is not legal for the local planning authority to 'sell' planning permission, and planning obligations should be negotiated in a way which makes it clear that this is not the intention.

MAKING THE FORMAL APPLICATION

A planning application is a formal written application. It usually consists of:

- A completed application form.
- A location plan showing the whereabouts of the application site.

- A site plan showing what is currently on the site, and what is proposed to be placed on it, except for applications concerned only with changes of use, etc.
- Floor plans and elevations of the proposed building, except where these are clearly not relevant.
- An ownership certificate, which confirms ownership details for the site. (This may be part of the application form.)
- An 'agricultural holdings certificate' (see below). (This too may be a part of the application form.)
- Usually (though this is not essential) a covering letter.
- Payment of the fee for the application (the local planning authority will confirm the fee payable).
- In some cases, supporting applications: for example, an application for listed building consent.
- For some applications – mostly large and sensitive industrial applications such as those for oil refineries, chemical works, and waste disposal incineration plants – it is necessary to draw up an environmental statement under the Environmental Impact Assessment regulations (see page 80).

THE APPLICATION FORM

Each local planning authority produces its own application form, though most of the elements are common to them all. Usually there are separate forms for residential and non-residential (that is, business and related) applications. Typically the form is two or three A4 pages in length. It provides space for the applicant to write in brief details of the application, but if the application is large and complex this will often need to be supplemented with additional information.

Of course, the form asks for standard details such as:

- the name and address of the applicant
- the address of the application site
- the applicant's interest in the site (for example, as owner or prospective purchaser)
- the type of permission being applied for (full, outline, renewal, etc.)
- brief details of the proposed change or development: both physical, and in terms of use class (see Chapter 2).

It will ask the applicant to detail the supporting information being provided, and for non-residential applications will generally ask at least brief questions about other aspects such as:

- the type of processes to be carried out in the building
- materials to be used
- drainage and sewage arrangements
- waste disposal arrangements
- the use or storage of hazardous substances
- traffic likely to be generated
- existing and future levels of employment
- parking arrangements.

THE SITE AND THE LOCATION PLAN

It is up to you as applicant to define the site to which the application relates. You need to provide a location plan which shows the site clearly, in the context of the surrounding area. (It should, for example, show the roads and buildings immediately surrounding the site.) You can buy an Ordnance Survey map and mark the site on this, or you may find it cheaper to ask the local planning authority to sell you a photocopied extract. Most will be happy to do this. Of course, you can also draw up a plan from scratch if you wish; but do

remember that OS and other published maps are copyright, and that you should avoid infringing the copyright by making an unauthorised copy, by hand or machine. A suitable scale for the location plan is 1:1,250 or 1:2,500. If you are using an existing map, you should make sure that it is up to date and that all significant roads, buildings and so on are included on it.

On the plan, you need to mark the boundary of the application site with a red line. The application site itself will often be the entire site which you own, have use of, or intend to acquire. Sometimes you might choose to exclude part of your site if there is to be no development on it. (Some of the fees for planning applications are determined on a scale basis depending on the size of the site.) If so, you need to make it clear on the site plan what area you own (by marking its boundary with a blue line. However, the site needs to include not only the location of any new or altered buildings, but also any area that is to be used for landscaping, car parking or vehicle access, if it is not already used for that purpose.

The site of the application can include land that you do not own or control, and in some circumstances it will need to do so: for example, to indicate how vehicle access will be provided.

THE SITE PLAN

This should be distinguished from the location plan. The location plan is intended to show where the site is in relation to its neighbourhood; the site plan shows what is currently on the site, and what is intended to be placed on the site as a result of the application. It needs to be at a larger scale, typically 1:500.

The site plan need not stop at the site boundary, though it will not extend too far beyond it. It should indicate:

- the site boundary and any changes in it as a result of the application
- rights of way across the site, if any
- buildings, existing and proposed
- buildings on adjoining land
- roads, pavements, verges and footpaths, both on and adjacent to the site, and any work that is to be done to them
- existing and proposed access (for pedestrians, cyclists, cars, delivery vehicles)
- parking areas
- existing trees and other significant natural features, and proposed landscaping
- existing and proposed drains, sewers, cesspools and septic tanks
- the uses to be made of parts of the site not being built on.

FLOOR PLANS AND ELEVATIONS

Full floor plans and elevations need to be drawn up if the application is for full permission and includes new buildings. These need to be of a professional standard, and properly to scale. They need not be drawn up by an architect, however; any competent technician can produce them. If the application is for a minor change to an existing building, it is not always necessary to draw up a full set of floor plans and elevations: for example, an application for a new sign on the front of the building would not require that floor plans be provided. However, for a full-scale application the elevations will need to show all sides of the building, and not merely the street frontage; the plans should show all floors, not just the ground floor.

It is important to distinguish existing build-

ings from proposed buildings, usually by shading any alterations or extensions.

The plans and elevations should be marked up to indicate features such as:

- the size and height of existing and proposed building(s)
- ground level, and any existing or proposed variation in it
- the design and layout, including details such as the positions of doors and windows
- materials and finishes, and the colour and texture of the exterior.

It can be helpful to provide a model of what is being proposed, or an artist's impression of the completed building. These are not legal requirements, but they are particularly useful if the building and its features are unusual, and would not necessarily be clear to development control committee members from a plan.

Plans for outline applications

It is not essential to provide such detail for an outline application. However, it is sometimes useful to include plans so as to convince officers and members that the site can accommodate the number and size of the buildings being applied for. In this case, the plans should be marked 'for illustrative purposes only', and the details on them will not be binding for the full application.

OWNERSHIP CERTIFICATES

It is not essential to own a site in order to apply for planning permission for it, but public policy dictates that the owner(s) should at least be aware of what is being proposed. Accordingly, applicants are required to complete an ownership certificate. There are four options:

- Certificate A: the applicant is the sole owner of the site, or the lessee of the entire site on a lease with more than seven years to run.
- Certificate B: the site is wholly or partly owned by someone else. The owner's name and address must be listed, and a notice of the application be sent to them.
- Certificate C: this option is used when you cannot identify all the site owners after taking all reasonable steps (including a newspaper advertisement). The applicant has to list the steps taken in detail, including the publication the advert was placed in, and the date.
- Certificate D: this is used when none of the owners can be identified. The same conditions apply as for Certificate C.

AGRICULTURAL HOLDINGS CERTIFICATES

There is a general presumption that agricultural land should not pass into other uses without careful review, and to this end it is a legal requirement that applicants fill in an 'agricultural holdings certificate' which states if any of the site is held under an agricultural tenancy. This applies everywhere, not just in rural areas. If any of the land is held by an agricultural tenant, then notice must be sent to them as part of the application process.

COVERING LETTERS

It is not essential to enclose a covering letter with the application, but it is good practice to do so, especially if you have had previous discussions with a planning officer, and want to address the application specifically to that person.

The letter should be brief and businesslike. As in personal discussions, you will want to choose carefully any points you make, to ensure that they enhance and do not negatively affect your case. If there are any plus points about the application that you feel have not been adequately covered on the application form, this is the place to emphasise them.

If you want to add additional factual information, it is probably better to enclose it as an addendum to the application form, rather than put it into the covering letter.

EXPIRY AND RENEWAL OF PLANNING PERMISSION

Planning permission is granted for a fixed period of time: usually five years, though this may be varied in the conditions of the permission. If you carry out the development within that time, the permission becomes permanent unless it has specifically been time-limited by condition (see page 48). You do not have to complete the development within the time limit, so long as you begin work. The legal position on what counts as implementing planning permission is complex, but generally case law has supported the view that any significant start to development (for example digging foundation trenches) is sufficient to count as implementing the permission.

If work has not started within the time limit then the permission expires, but you can apply to have it renewed. You might also apply for renewal:

- if reserved matters had not been resolved within three years of outline planning permission being granted
- if permission was granted for a limited period and you wanted to extend the period or make the permission permanent.

You can normally assume that renewal will be granted unless there has been a material change in circumstances. However, 'material changes in circumstances' can include changes to the policy framework, as well as changes on your site, or in the surrounding area, so renewal is not automatic.

An application for renewal is made in the same form as the original application for planning permission. In general, the same information needs to be provided.

RESERVED MATTERS APPLICATIONS

These are the issues which need to be agreed before outline planning permission is converted into full permission. Proposals on the reserved matters need to be submitted within three years of the grant of outline permission. Normally a further fee is not payable.

You can apply for determination of reserved matters, either on a standard application form, or by letter. In both cases, of course, you will need to provide full details, which will usually include a site plan, and floor plans and elevations. If you wish, you can submit several alternative reserved matters applications, and only decide at a later stage which is to be combined with the outline permission to form the basis of your full planning permission.

The reserved matters application need not be made by the applicant who obtained outline permission, and often is not: for example, when a landowner obtains outline permission before selling a site, and the purchaser carries out the development.

KEY POINTS

✔ *Most planning applications are determined by 'district level' planning authorities, but applications for waste disposal, mineral extraction and some other types are determined on a 'county' level.*

✔ *It is not a requirement that you obtain expert help, but you will probably find it necessary for all but very small applications.*

✔ *You do not have to consult the local planning authority before (or after) submitting your application, but unless it is very simple and straightforward, it will probably benefit you to do so.*

✔ *You can consult either officers (professional planners) or members (elected councillors), or both, if you wish.*

✔ *Your application may only be approved if you accept conditions to it, or enter into a planning obligation. It is as well to discuss these issues at an early stage.*

✔ *Your application will need to be accompanied by a location plan, a more detailed site plan, and floor plans and elevations for proposed new buildings.*

✔ *Planning permission is finite, but if it is not implemented within the time limit you can apply for it to be renewed.*

✔ *If you wish to implement outline planning permission, you first need to turn it into full permission by submitting a reserved matters application.*

CHAPTER 5

The environment and its users

This chapter considers some specific issues which you may need to take into account in preparing your development proposal. You will need to do this in order to:

- gain all the benefits of planning your development in a socially responsible and environmentally sustainable way
- help ensure that you take into account the needs of your workforce and your customers, and
- ensure that you comply with national policies and maximise the chance of your proposal receiving planning approval.

The issues considered in this chapter include:

- the choice of sites for commercial activities
- development in rural areas
- flood risk
- transport issues
- parking
- access for the disabled
- security issues.

CHOOSING SITES FOR COMMERCIAL ACTIVITIES

Among the government's concerns in setting the planning policy framework are:

- Ensuring that 'brownfield' (previously developed) sites are reused and that 'greenfield' (never developed) land, and particularly agricultural and amenity land, is preserved.

- Ensuring that existing buildings are conserved and reused where appropriate.

- Promoting the vitality of existing commercial centres.

- Protecting the amenity of rural areas (which includes not only conserving the natural environment, but also ensuring that commercial services and employment opportunities are retained and where necessary developed).

- Ensuring that private development echoes the pattern of the existing and developing public infrastructure.
- Encouraging competition.
- And, of course, ensuring that development is planned and implemented with a view to the principles of sustainability.

The framework that results is concerned with designating both broad areas and, in some cases, specific sites for specific types of development (as we showed in Chapter 2). If you are considering a location for a commercial or industrial development, it is essential that you take account of the pattern of designation in your region and in your local area.

Where commercial activity is concerned, the general trend is to designate a hierarchy of centres in each area: from major centres serving the entire region, to smaller centres serving an area within the region, to local and rural centres serving a small town or village. Planners look to ensure that new development fits this pattern, and is directed to centres at an appropriate level. Obviously, different types of shop are more suited to different levels of centre, and a large supermarket or a furniture store, which would be appropriate in a town, would be far less appropriate in a small village centre.

In general planners give most favour to proposals that are firmly and appropriately located within existing centres, and tend to look with less favour at proposals for sites on the fringes of existing centres, and with positive disfavour on proposals that do not fit the pattern of centres at all. The hierarchy of preference is:

- town centre sites
- edge-of-centre sites

- out-of-centre sites in locations that are (or will be) well served by public transport
- out-of-centre sites without prospects of adequate public transport.

What this means in practice is that developers are expected to show that they have looked at all available town centre sites, before they will be permitted to develop a less central site for a commercial use that would best belong in a town centre.

The three key tests that are applied to each site, according to government guidelines (*Planning Policy Guidance* note 6, on *Town Centres and Retail Developments*) are:

- the impact of development on the site on the vitality and viability of town centres
- its accessibility by a choice of means of transport
- the impact of development on the overall pattern of travel and car use.

Green belts continue to be an essential part of the policy framework, and there is a general presumption against development in these areas.

Because the current policy framework is so firmly oriented to using retail development to help strengthen and, where necessary, regenerate existing town centres, the trend at the moment is against approving proposals for out-of-town shopping centres of the kind that were much more welcome in the 1970s, 1980s and early 1990s. Although these are often relatively cheap to develop, they tend to have a negative effect on existing centres, and to create pressure for development of the road network in a way which is generally thought to be undesirable. The same policy now applies to major entertainment facilities: out-of-town complexes of cinemas, bowling alleys, night-clubs and the like. The presumption is that these facilities, too, should be located in existing centres.

However, where it is felt that there is a clear need for developments that would generate a substantial amount of traffic, which is too large to be accommodated in or on the edge of town centres, it is sometimes an option to combine them with existing out-of-centre developments and to negotiate for improvements to their accessibility by public transport. This is typically done by entering into a planning agreement, as outlined on page 48. Developers are, however, expected to prove first that all available central sites have been considered.

Although it is a priority to locate commercial development in existing centres, it is also seen as a possible danger that large single-use developments might overwhelm an area and cause it to lose rather than gain vitality. Accordingly, another policy trend is towards encouraging mixed-use developments: for example, developments which combine shops, offices and housing on a single large site. These developments are perhaps more popular with planners than they are with developers, and local authorities are invited by government policy to 'take a flexible approach' in encouraging them, for example, by relaxing their usual guidelines about the amount of parking that would be allowed on site.

DEVELOPMENT IN RURAL AREAS

Although the presumption is that rural areas should be protected from 'unnecessary' development, this does not mean that there is a ban on any development in rural areas (although greater restrictions can be expected in areas of great biodiversity or landscape value). Planners do accept that residents in, and tourists to, rural areas are in need of services, and they positively encourage the vitality of village, as well as of city, centres.

The presumption is that what development is allowed in rural areas should be primarily within the boundary of (or a minor extension to) existing settlements, and that there should not be development in other locations without good reason. Agricultural land can be developed only exceptionally, and where it is under consideration, the quality of the land (from an agricultural viewpoint) is a significant issue.

It is a policy however to encourage commercial development of a suitable scale in rural areas, and local planning authorities are expected to encourage small businesses especially to find appropriate sites, even where land has not specifically been designated for employment uses. Where buildings were originally built for industrial or commercial use, their refurbishment for new industrial and commercial uses is generally favoured (and their conversion to residential use less favoured).

It is accepted that in rural areas it is not practicable to look for the same level of accessibility by public transport as can be found in urban areas, and this is taken into account in assessing applications for commercial or industrial developments. They are expected to be located in 'comparatively' rather than perfectly accessible locations.

Recent guidance has particularly encouraged 'appropriate' development to meet the needs of tourists, but this development is expected to be proportional in scale (a huge hotel would not generally be the answer in a small country village), and to be of a design that is of a high standard and appropriate to its environment.

HOLIDAY ACCOMMODATION

'Holiday occupancy' conditions are seen as one way of trying to balance the need for good-quality tourist accommodation with the need to avoid over-development in rural areas. This is a condition attached to planning permission, which specifies that the development must not be used by permanent residents. Sometimes the condition specifies that the accommodation can only be used during a fixed holiday season, but this is not always the case: if the accommodation is suitable for winter use, for example, and there is no overriding reason why this is thought undesirable, then all-round residency can be permitted.

One argument for this distinction is that holidaymakers can be expected to use the local infrastructure less than do permanent residents: for example, they will not send their children to local schools, use medical facilities except on an emergency basis, or make major purchases such as furniture. Tests such as whether children attend local schools can be used to assess whether the accommodation is being used in accordance with the planning condition.

In some cases, planners permit the conversion of redundant agricultural and other rural buildings into holiday accommodation, where they would not permit conversion to permanent residential dwellings. It is also argued that this reduces the overall pressure on the housing supply in rural areas.

CAMPING AND CARAVAN SITES

Caravan sites need both planning permission and a site licence (under the Caravan Sites and Control of Development Act 1960), although there are a small number of exceptions (for example, caravanning organisations are permitted to certify small sites (less than five vans) for use only by their members). Planning permission for caravan sites is sometimes given with a condition limiting the amount of the year for which the site is open, but the current government guidelines encourage local planning authorities to relax these conditions where possible. It is not always necessary to get permission in order to run a tent-based campsite. If it is used for less than 28 days per year, it can fall under the permitted development guidelines, and no site licence is needed if it is open for periods of less than 42 days, or for fewer than 60 days in total each year.

FLOODING

LAND AT RISK
About 8 per cent of the total area of land in England is at risk of being flooded by rivers. Another 1.5 per cent is at risk from flooding by the sea. In total, about 1.3 million homes and businesses face a significant flood risk.

Climate change is increasing the susceptibility of land to flooding, and also increasing the challenge faced by the Environment Agency (EA), which has responsibility for dealing with flood defences. Flood risk is a material planning permission, and the government stance is that since much built-up land is already subject to risk, defences should be concentrated on these areas, and there should be a presumption against new development in particularly flood-prone areas.

The EA is a statutory consultee on planning applications, and will advise the local planning authority to add conditions, or to refuse permission, if a proposed development is at too much risk from flooding. This can also happen if it is thought liable to alter drainage patterns and thus increase the flood risk on other property. The EA provides advice on flood prevention, to individuals as well as local planning authorities, and should be consulted if you suspect your development site is at risk of flooding. In some cases a development becomes feasible only if flood defences are provided, not necessarily on the development site itself, but on a neighbouring site. One option is for the developer to offer to enter into a planning obligation to contribute to the cost of the area defences.

TRANSPORT AND ROAD SAFETY

Whether your proposed development site is in an inner city or in a remote rural area, transport will be an issue that affects it. Planners will look carefully both at the available modes of transport for staff, suppliers and customers, and at the effect that any increase in traffic will have on the neighbourhood more generally. They will also look at parking provision – an issue discussed below. This is clearly a particular concern when you are selecting a site for a new development, but you may also find transport-related issues affecting the ways in which development is permitted on existing sites.

Green transport plans

It is a good idea for every business to draw up a green transport plan, and for new developments it can be a requirement of planning

permission that one is drawn up (and of course, adhered to). The aim of the green plan is to analyse the modes of transport used by those coming to the site (suppliers, staff and customers) and to plan the development of the transport uses in a way that minimises congestion, pollution and energy usage. Issues covered might include, for instance:

- the improvement of routes for staff and customers to walk to the premises
- cycle routes to and on the site, and other provision such as cycle parking, lockers, and showers for those cycling to work
- facilities for public transport and its users: for example, bays for buses to park in, and bus shelters
- support for, or participation in, local park and ride schemes.

Road safety and congestion issues

There are two levels of highway authority with control over public roads:

- The Secretary of State is responsible for motorways and trunk roads.
- County-level local authorities (including unitary authorities and London boroughs) are responsible for all other highways.

Local planning authorities – and their consultees, the highway authorities – are particularly concerned with the safety of access points and will look carefully at how access to and from the development has been laid out. In some cases, the existing road layout will not be adequate to cope with a new development. In this case, it is an option for the local planning authority to ask the developer to enter into a planning obligation to fund improvements to the highway system. The agreement might include, for example, the provision of new traffic lights to control traffic into a significant new development.

Planning application forms ask questions about the estimated vehicle flow to the premises, usually separated out into goods, staff and customers. As well as looking at the overall amount of traffic, the local planning authority may be concerned about hours of delivery, for example, or may place conditions to ensure that deliveries only take place at times when the transport system can cope with them.

Of course, the amount of road congestion that is created depends in large part on *how* people and goods reach the site, and here planners look with particular care at the level of public transport provision.

Public transport

There are no fixed guidelines about the degree of accessibility by public transport that is required for any particular size of development. It depends entirely on circumstances, and clearly less accessibility is expected for a development in a rural area than for one in a city centre. However, as we noted above, there is a presumption that development will take place in conformance with the developing road and public transport network, and in a way that conforms with green transport guidelines. Should a developer obtain permission to site a commercial development in a location not well served by public transport, the local planning authority will almost certainly look to the developer to fund improvements to its public transport accessibility. (This could consist, for example, of subsidising a bus from the nearest centre to the development site.)

Parking

Sustainable development policies generally look to minimise private car use, as we have shown, and a suitable parking strategy is seen as one way of helping to achieve this. Some studies have suggested that levels of parking provision are more important than levels of public transport provision in determining whether people drive to work. Accordingly, the current policy trend is to discourage excessive car-parking provision, especially for staff, who should be encouraged to come to work by other means of transport wherever this is practicable. 'Car-free housing' is also encouraged in city centres. No such limitation applies to safe cycle parking provision, which is almost always encouraged.

For larger developments this translates into guidelines about the maximum amount of car parking which should be permitted in a new development, depending on the type of use. These guidelines do not apply to smaller planning applications which fall under the thresholds.

MAXIMUM PARKING STANDARDS

These are guidelines as to the maximum amount of parking provision which is likely to be allowed in new developments.

Use	Maximum no of spaces	Size of development above which this applies
Food retail	1 per 18–20 m²	1,000 m²
Non-food retail	1 per 20–22 m²	1,000 m²
Cinemas and conference facilities	1 per 5 seats	1,000 m²
D2 uses including leisure	1 per 22–25 m²	1,000 m²
B1 uses including offices	1 per 35 m²	2,500 m²

Local planning authorities do, however, accept that while employees should be discouraged from driving to work, there is a need for some parking provision in commercial centres, particularly for short-term users such as shoppers. Without this parking provision the centre may not flourish, and there may be a 'perverse' incentive for developers to move to out-of-centre sites, which is not the intention of the policy.

The main need is seen to be for parking which serves the centre as a whole, rather than dedicated parking for individual developments, and in some cases local planning authorities may look to enter into planning obligations in which individual developers contribute to the cost of providing off-site parking facilities.

There is a particular need for parking spaces for the disabled, and for others in priority groups such as parents with small children. If your development includes parking provision, you may be required to designate some spaces for these purposes, as well as for visitors rather than staff.

Where public transport to a development site is initially limited, but is expected to improve, local planning authorities sometimes impose a condition that the initial amount of parking provided on site should be reduced when the public transport provision comes on stream.

One favoured policy at present is the shared use of parking spaces: for instance, by shoppers in the daytime and then for users of leisure facilities at night, and proposals on these lines are particularly welcome by local planning authorities.

ACCESS ISSUES

Government policies are increasingly concerned with the inclusion of minorities into community life, and developers are obliged to take account of the needs for access of the disabled to public places and to workspaces. The internal layout of buildings is not normally a consideration for planners, and is instead covered by building regulations: Part M of Schedule 1 to the Building Regulations 1991 lays out the requirements on developers to provide access inside buildings. These include an avoidance of unnecessary changes in level, and the provision of lifts and disabled lavatories.

External layout issues are an issue for local planning authorities, and planning officers look to see that disabled access is properly catered for. The issues here include, for example:

- the provision of level access into shops and other commercial premises, so that they are accessible to wheelchair users
- the provision of disabled parking places close to access points
- paths and other access routes designed with the needs of the disabled (including the blind and deaf and those with mental handicaps) in mind
- general safety considerations which apply to the mentally and physically disadvantaged.

These guidelines apply to the conversion of existing buildings, as well as to new build. Developers, and planning authorities, are expected to be 'flexible and imaginative' in looking for solutions.

When a design for a development is submitted without sufficient regard to access issues, the local planning authority may place a condition on it, requiring better access for people with disabilities.

SECURITY ISSUES

The security of your building is perhaps of more concern to you than it is to your planning authority, since it is your business that could be the target of crime. However, the building's design and its external lighting also affect security in the surrounding neighbourhood.

The right design can help to reduce the vulnerability of your premises, so it is important to take account of security considerations right at the outset. Police crime-prevention officers provide free advice, and it is well worth consulting them.

These are some points to take into account:

- Look carefully at possible unauthorised access points, for example, a flat-roofed extension could give easier access to upstairs windows, or a new window near a drainpipe could be used for access.

- If you are extending your premises, you may also need to extend your alarm system.

- Good lighting at night enhances the image of your premises, acts as an advertisement for your business, and also deters unauthorised visitors or intruders. It is important to ensure that the lighting respects the needs of your neighbours, and does not, for example, glare into their windows. Overly strong lights can be a security drawback as they create blind spots and shadowed areas.

- Buildings that are visible to others – passing pedestrians and traffic, and occupants of nearby premises – are less vulnerable than secluded buildings. Careful siting and landscaping can improve the visibility of your premises, and thus their security.

- Avoid providing hiding places such as recessed doorways.

- Ensure that you use hard-wearing materials which will not deteriorate to provide weak points in your building. A well-maintained building is less vulnerable than one which appears run-down.

KEY POINTS

✔ *If you are planning a commercial development, you need to look initially at sites in existing centres. Planners are unlikely to approve a development on an out-of-centre site if a more central one is available.*

✔ *Development can take place in rural areas, but it is carefully controlled and mostly confined to existing settlements.*

✔ *It can be acceptable to provide holiday accommodation in circumstances where new permanent housing would not get planning approval.*

✔ *There is a presumption against development in areas which are subject to flooding.*

✔ *It is a good idea to draw up a green transport plan for your business, and sometimes a requirement to do so.*

✔ *Road safety issues are an important aspect of any planning proposal.*

✔ *Your application is more likely to be approved if the site has good accessibility by foot, cycle and public transport.*

✔ *Car parking for staff is generally discouraged; car parking for customers can be provided within guidelines.*

✔ *Dedicated car-parking provision is less favoured than provision open to the centre as a whole, and shared-use parking is a particularly good option.*

✔ *You must consider access for disabled people, both inside your building and elsewhere on your site.*

✔ *Look to design in security. The police and your local crime-prevention panel can provide advice.*

CHAPTER 6

How planning applications are handled

Chapter 4 covered the process of making a planning application. This chapter looks in more detail at what happens to the application after it has been submitted. Once you have read it you should understand:

- how consultation takes place, and what impact objections have
- why and how applications are delegated to planning staff for consideration
- how revisions to applications are negotiated
- what happens in the development control committee meeting
- how to appeal against refusal of permission, and
- how to refer mishandling to the local government ombudsman.

THE CONSULTATION PROCESS

Basically, three types of consultation are carried out once your planning application is submitted:

- Statutory consultees have a legal right to comment on the application, and in some cases to direct the local planning authority to attach conditions or to refuse the application. They include:
  - the British Waterways Board
  - the Civil Aviation Authority
  - the Coal Authority
  - English Heritage (and equivalent bodies elsewhere in the UK)
  - English Nature (and equivalent groups)
  - the Environment Agency and its equivalents
  - the Greater London Authority (for applications in Greater London)
  - the Health and Safety Executive
  - the Highways Agency
  - local highway authorities
  - the Department of the Environment, Food and Rural Affairs
  - parish and community councils
  - the police (who advise on crime prevention issues).
- Voluntary consultees are bodies which

have asked to be informed of certain classes of, or all, planning applications. They include local amenity and heritage groups, and lobbying organisations such as environmental groups and cycling groups.

- The public are also advised of applications through advertisements and site notices, or by the serving of a notice on the site's neighbours, and have a right to make representations about them.

How consultation takes place

The local planning authority normally sends information on planning applications it has received automatically to statutory and voluntary consultees with an interest in the application. Not all consultees will be interested in all applications. For example, English Heritage is interested primarily in applications affecting listed buildings and scheduled ancient monuments, the Highways Agency in applications affecting traffic on, or access points to and from, trunk roads while parish councils will be interested only in applications in their parish, and so on. It is up to the local planning authority to choose the format in which the information is sent out: for example, they might opt to send a list of all applications automatically, and to provide further information on request.

The local planning authority also has a statutory duty to publicise planning applications. This is done:

- through notices in the local press
- through the issuance of committee agendas, a few days before the meeting is scheduled to take place
- and through the erection of site notices.

The general public often learn about applications in this way, though they may also learn about them through editorial coverage in local media, or by word of mouth; or you as applicant may choose to discuss your proposals directly with your neighbours and anyone else likely to be affected by them.

Site notices

Site notices (formal notices advising that an application has been submitted, posted in a visible location on or near the site boundary) are a legal requirement for many (though not all) types of application. If they are legally required, the local planning authority is obliged to erect them. Some local planning authorities have voluntary schemes for circumstances where site notices are not essential, whereby applicants are sent notices and asked to post them up. By displaying a notice, you alert neighbours to your proposal, and of course run the risk that they will object to it. However, if the proposal goes ahead they are certain to learn of it at some stage, so it is usually best to prepare to face objections early on, and in this sense it is to your advantage to display a notice.

The timescale for consultation

By law local planning authorities must allow at least 14 days for the consultation process, although most authorities set 21- or 28-day deadlines.

The format for responding

There is no set rule about how responses should be phrased. Sometimes the local planning authority's consultation form provides directly for brief feedback, but it is open to either formal consultees or the public to write in and make their comments in whatever form they wish. Consultees can either support or object to the application, and/or make comments suggesting improvements or requesting (or for some statutory consultees, requiring) that conditions be applied.

Consultees can only object validly on planning grounds. Other grounds for objection – for example, that their own property will be devalued if the application is approved, that they will lose a view they value, or that the enterprise will offer competition which they would prefer not to face – are not valid and the development control committee will be instructed to ignore them. Objections on legitimate grounds might, for instance, consist of:

- Objections that the proposal is not in accordance with the local or structure plan: for example, new housing is proposed in an area which is not within the settlement boundary.
- An objection to the size, or (in broad terms) the design, of a proposal because it is not considered suitable for the individual site or the surrounding neighbourhood.
- An objection from neighbours whom the proposal would disadvantage for legitimate reasons (in planning terms): for example, loss of light to their windows, the impact of noise or smell from the new enterprise, or disturbance from increased traffic flow.
- Comments from lobbying bodies about their specific interests: for example, a cycling group might press for better provision of cycle routes or cycle parking.
- Objections that the infrastructure (water supply, sewage, local facilities) is inadequate to handle the development.
- Concerns about road safety (for example, cars turning into a main road from an inadequately sighted access point).

Finding out if there are objections

If you are concerned that there may be objections to your application, you can contact the local planning authority to enquire, at around the expiry of the consultation period. The planning officer handling the application will be able to tell you if any have been received. He or she should also tell you what comments have been received from statutory consultees, and the substance of objections from individuals. However, the personal details of individuals writing in to comment are normally kept confidential until the officer's report is issued shortly before the development control meeting.

Reacting to objections

You have three options if your proposal has attracted objections:

- You can choose to ignore the objections in the hope that your application will be approved in spite of them. You might well do this, for example, if the planning officer had recommended approval in his or her report (see page 65).
- You can revise your proposal to try to meet the objections. There is no additional fee for doing this. If you plan to do so, it is worth advising the planning officer so that your application will not be considered until your revisions have been received.
- You can discuss the objections with the objectors and try to persuade them that they are not justified in their concerns. You may feel it is worth doing this if you are able to gauge who has objected from the comments, or if objections have come from a local body such as the parish council. It is rather less feasible to counter the objections of a national consultee.

If you persuade an objector to withdraw their objection, either by discussing the proposal with them or by modifying it, then you will need to ask them to contact the local planning authority and advise it that the objection has been withdrawn.

A hearing for consultees

All consultees, statutory or voluntary, and all organisations and individuals who submit comments, are assured that their comments will be taken into account, provided the comments are valid in planning terms. This is not always in detail: for example, the planning officer's report to committee might refer briefly to the fact that there have been, say, six letters in support of the proposal, and the application may be discussed without further reference to them. (The letters will however be available for members and the public to read on request.) Research has shown that the majority of consultees felt their views were taken into account, though consultees complained that there was inadequate feedback for them to be certain of this. (Consultees are not routinely informed of the result of the application.)

The fact that there are objections is not of itself an argument for rejecting an application, although it may carry informal weight with members. The issue is whether the objectors (or supporters) raise valid points in planning terms.

DELEGATED DECISIONS

Not all planning applications are considered by a development control committee. Some are determined by planning officers under *delegated powers*. Each local planning authority has the right to decide the criteria by which decisions on applications are delegated to offi-

cers, but applications determined under delegated powers, are usually relatively minor applications which have not received any objections.

It is not usual for applications to be refused under delegated powers. If the recommendation is for refusal, the application will be considered by a committee of councillors.

As well as decisions being delegated to officers without the application going to a committee, sometimes the development control committee itself delegates the final decision on applications it has considered. This is sometimes done:

- When the application is considered shortly before the expiry of the consultation period, and the committee is minded to approve it. (This is often done to try to ensure that applications are determined within the government's target time of eight weeks.) If no objections are received by the deadline, the application will then be approved.
- When further information of a technical kind is needed, such as details of the drainage scheme, and the committee are minded to approve the application provided this is satisfactory.
- When small revisions are required, and the development control committee consider it unnecessary to review them in detail.
- When a planning obligation agreement (see page 48) needs drawing up before formal approval is given.

THE PLANNING OFFICER'S REPORT TO COMMITTEE

The agenda for the development control committee meeting, at which your application will be discussed, is a public document. It should be made available at least three clear days

65

before the meeting. You can obtain a copy on request from the local planning authority's offices, but the local planning authority is unlikely to send you a copy automatically, or indeed to advise you of the date of the meeting unless you ask.

The agenda will be accompanied by planning officers' reports and recommendations on all the applications to be considered. All papers are made public unless they meet strict criteria which justify their remaining confidential. Letters from objectors, and supporters, will not automatically be included with the agenda (although, in practice, they often will be), but they should be available for review on request. It is not normally possible for those commenting to remain anonymous at this stage, and you may well want to know their identity, as will the committee, since issues such as the closeness of their premises to your application site may be relevant.

The report on your application will summarise it briefly, comment on its suitability and conformance or otherwise with the policy framework, report on the outcome of consultations, and make a recommendation (which may include conditions to be attached if the recommendation is for approval). A location plan is often appended, but it is not usual for your site plans and elevations to be attached; they will however be made available at the meeting.

Whatever the officer's recommendation, you should not assume that the committee will automatically accept it. In the majority of cases it is accepted, but it is quite common for the recommendation to be overturned by the committee, and at least as common for the committee to attach conditions which the officer had not initially recommended. The com-

mittee does not have to give its reasons if it approves an application, but if it refuses the application then it must justify that refusal *on planning grounds*.

Read the report carefully. If there are any inaccuracies, contact the planning officer immediately to point them out. If they are serious, and you feel they have affected the recommendation, then it is worth your while to also contact the chair of the committee, or your local councillor.

If the recommendation is for approval without conditions

You will of course be pleased if this is the case, but you should still check carefully, and should certainly not take it for granted that the application will be approved.

If the recommendation is for approval with conditions

If the conditions are acceptable to you, this will not be a problem. If the conditions are not acceptable to you, you will need to consider your next course of action. You could:

- leave the application to be considered, and appeal afterwards for variation of the conditions
- lobby to have the conditions amended (see below for how to do this)
- withdraw the application for further consideration and perhaps revision.

If the recommendation is for refusal

Do not despair, particularly if the reasons for refusal do not seem particularly strong to you. The options are the same as those above.

Revising the application

You can still do this, even at a late stage, if it seems advisable. As was mentioned earlier, if you plan to revise the application, let the planning officer know in good time so it can be withdrawn from consideration.

If you feel you would much prefer the original application to any revised form, however, there is no real disadvantage in letting the committee consider the original. If it's approved, all to the good; if it's refused, you can still revise it and resubmit.

If you make substantial revisions, the local planning authority may decide it is necessary to re-publicise and consult over the application.

Whether your application is considered and refused or withdrawn before formal consideration, you do not have to pay an additional fee for a revised application that is submitted within a year of the original application.

Lobbying before the meeting

- If you are worried about factual inaccuracies in the report, then the best person to contact is the officer with whom you have been dealing.
- If you are worried about objectors, then it may be worth contacting them directly, and discussing their concerns with them. You may be able to persuade them to withdraw the objection, or you may see your way to revising the application so as to meet their objection.
- If you feel that the officer's recommendation is wrong, either because he or she has recommended refusal without very strong reasons, or because he or she has recommended conditions which are unacceptable to you, the best person to approach is often a councillor. You can approach the chair or vice chair of the committee, all members of the committee, or a local ward councillor (who need not be a member of the committee, but should be willing to put your case, or to suggest another councillor who will do so).

You can:

- phone or e-mail the individuals you wish to contact
- or lobby individuals in writing before the meeting (though you may have to deliver your letters by hand, since the timescale will be tight)
- or submit representations in writing, asking that these be put before the committee
- or ask to speak at the committee meeting (see below)
- or ask a councillor to put your case for you (see below).

THE DEVELOPMENT CONTROL MEETING

Development control meetings are normally open to the public. You are not obliged to attend as applicant, but you can attend if you wish. The meeting may last for several hours. The committee clerk who handles arrangements should be able to advise you roughly when your application will be considered, if you do not want to sit through the entire meeting. If timing is a real problem for you, you can ask whether your application can be considered at a fixed time, but the chair will have to weigh your request against other similar requests and the need for the meeting to proceed smoothly, and may not always agree.

Today, applicants are normally permitted to speak in the course of the debate on their application, although this was not the case until recently. (This is an area in which Human Rights legislation is likely to have an impact.) If you do wish to speak, it is as well to make that clear in advance to either the chair, the committee clerk, or the planning officer you have been dealing with. Particularly if your application is large, and/or you have a model or drawings to show, you could ask to present it to members yourself, or have your agent do so, before the planning officer goes through his or her report. Alternatively, you could ask to be allowed to make your comments in the course of the debate. Whichever is the case, it is good practice to introduce yourself to the committee clerk and the chair before the meeting begins.

If you do not feel comfortable about addressing the committee, you can ask a councillor to make representations on your behalf. Normally you will ask a councillor who represents your own ward to do this for you, whether or not he or she is a member of the committee. It would not be appropriate to ask the chair to state your case. A councillor whom you brief to do this should put your case conscientiously, but he or she need not necessarily agree with it, and if he or she is a committee member, you cannot reasonably object if he/she makes points on his/her own behalf that conflict with your case, or votes against approval.

The length of debate on individual applications varies from a few minutes to hours. If the application is straightforward, the debate will usually end with an immediate decision on the application. The chair may not take a formal vote on this if the committee's view is clear. If the committee are not prepared to accept the application without revisions, they may

choose to defer a decision so that these can be negotiated. Depending on the scale of the revisions, the revised application might either be brought to the next meeting, or be delegated for officers to approve. If issues arise that warrant it, the committee members can also defer the decision to give them an opportunity to make a site visit, which could be either a formal committee visit, or an informal visit from one or more members.

Councillors with an interest in the application

Any committee member with an interest in your application is required by local government guidelines to state this fact at the meeting. 'Interest' is not clearly defined, so this is partly a matter of judgment. If the councillor has met you in passing, this would not ordinarily count as an interest, although if the meeting was specifically to discuss your application, the councillor would need to declare that fact; but if he or she is a close personal friend, this could reasonably be considered as an interest. A councillor expressing an interest will not take any part in the decision on your application. If the interest is substantial – for example, a financial interest in your company, or a near blood relationship – then the councillor is usually required to withdraw from the meeting.

The interest need not be directly in your business: committee members would also be regarded as being interested if they were closely involved with – or were themselves – neighbours to the proposed development, or people otherwise likely to be substantially affected by it, such as your business rivals.

The onus is on the member him/herself to declare the interest, and act as appropriate.

often following legal advice from the local planning authority's staff. If however you are aware of a member's interest which you feel should have been declared and has not been, then you might choose to bring this discreetly to the attention of the chair or the committee clerk. Failure to declare a clear and substantial interest, if this affects the outcome of the application, would be considered as maladministration on the council's behalf, and you have redress via the local government ombudsman (see below).

NON-DETERMINATION

It is often very frustrating for applicants if their application is not decided at the development control meeting, and sometimes it causes serious difficulties with the scheduling of the development. However, committees usually only defer applications if the alternative is refusal, so it is rarely wise to press for an immediate decision.

If your application has not been determined within eight weeks of submission, you have the option of appealing on the grounds of non-determination. This follows the appeals procedure discussed below. However, the appeals process is itself quite slow, so there is rarely an advantage in doing so if your application is making slow but reasonable progress. You would only do so if it was completely deadlocked for some reason. There is a six-month time limit on appeals, so you might choose to do this if the limit was approaching.

THE DECISION NOTICE

You do not have formal planning permission until the planning officer has issued a decision notice to you. This should be done shortly after the development control meeting. If you do not receive it within a week, it is advisable to chase up.

REASONS FOR REFUSAL

As was mentioned earlier, development control committees do not have to give their reasons for approving an application, even if it appears to be contrary to planning policy. However, if the application is refused, then all the reasons for its refusal must be given in writing.

The reasons given must be on planning grounds, of the kind that were outlined earlier in the book. Non-planning grounds – including personal dislike of the design, or the strength of local opposition to the proposals, if this has not been substantiated in planning terms – are not valid as reasons for refusal.

APPEALING AGAINST REFUSAL OR AGAINST CONDITIONS

Who can appeal

If your planning application has been refused, you have the right to appeal against the decision. You do not have to show good reason in order to make an appeal, but of course unless you can justify (on planning grounds) your request to have the decision overturned, your appeal is most unlikely to be successful. Only the applicant can appeal. If an earlier planning application on a site in which you are interested was refused, and you want to revive it, then you must reapply from scratch.

It is not possible for an objector to appeal against approval of planning permission. If you as an objector feel that there are overriding reasons why permission should not have been granted, you may however have a case to raise with the local government ombudsman (see below); but the ombudsman does not have the power to overturn the planning approval, and can, at best, only suggest alternative remedies.

Appealing to the High Court is also a rather last-ditch alternative (see below).

APPEALS

- about 15,000 appeals against refusal of planning permission (or against conditions attached to approval) are made each year
- about one-third of all appeals are allowed.

Who to appeal to

Appeals in England are heard by a planning inspector who is a member of the Planning Inspectorate, a quango, and is nominally appointed by the Secretary of State. In Scotland, appeals are made to the Scottish Ministers and usually delegated to the Scottish Executive Inquiry Reporters Unit.

The timing of appeals

It is necessary to lodge your appeal within six months from issue of the decision notice. If you are appealing against non-determination of your application (see above), then the appeal must be made within six months plus eight weeks of the date of the application.

Appealing is a relatively slow process. As a general guideline, you and the local planning authority are expected to submit written representations to the planning inspector within four months of the appeal being lodged. You can expect a decision on your appeal about nine months after you lodge it.

The cost of appealing

There is no fee for appealing. However, your appeal is unlikely to be successful unless you submit a strong case, and it will take time and trouble to prepare that case. Your costs cannot normally be recovered, even if your appeal is successful. In some circumstances the local planning authority might be awarded costs against you, though this would not be done if you had reasonable grounds for making an appeal.

Types of appeal

There are three different procedures for appealing. It is up to you to suggest which procedure you wish to use, although your choice can be overruled in some circumstances.

Written representations

This is the simplest procedure, and 80 per cent of appeals are handled this way. You, as applicant, and the local planning authority draw up statements which are sent to the planning inspector. You can send in a full statement initially, or you can begin by submitting a brief summary of the grounds for your appeal, and wait to see the local planning authority's statement before submitting your own in full. Each side has a chance to reply to points made by the other side. The inspector then makes a site visit and issues a decision, which has immediate effect and cannot readily be overturned. A decision to grant your appeal is effectively the same as a grant of planning permission.

Informal hearings

These are normally used for larger and more complex applications. They demand more from you in terms of professional knowledge, so although you are not legally obliged to seek expert help, you would be well advised to do so if you take this route. The applicant and the local planning authority exchange statements as before, then the planning inspector states which issues she or he wants to discuss at a hearing. The inspector generally makes a site visit, and there is an informal meeting at which both sides and the inspector have the opportunity to ask questions and make points.

Public inquiries

A public inquiry is a major undertaking, so this process is usually reserved for applications of very large scale. Inquiries are often called when either side expects there to be substantial third-party interest: for example, in an application for a major shopping development on a greenfield site, or a large factory on an environmentally sensitive site. If the Secretary of State judges it desirable, he or she can override a request for a simpler appeal and call a public inquiry.

The sides at a public inquiry are usually legally represented, and are expected to call expert witnesses, so this is a very expensive procedure for all involved.

The reasons for your appeal

Your reasons for appeal must be valid in planning terms, but they do not have to be limited to the grounds for refusal given on the decision notice. You can raise other arguments in your favour, and it is open to the local planning authority to raise new objections to your proposal when you first appeal. However, all the main arguments have to be stated at the outset of the appeal, and it is not normally allowable for either side to introduce entirely new arguments later in the process.

Bodies involved in an appeal

As well as the applicant and the local planning authority, other bodies with an interest in the appeal can also appear at an appeal inquiry. Those taking an interest might include local

councils who are not the local planning authority (including parish councils), national bodies who were statutory consultees to the original application, and others who objected to the original application.

CHALLENGING THE APPEAL DECISION

You can only challenge the appeal decision if you feel it is wrong on a point of law or if the proper procedure has not been followed. Challenges must be made through the High Court, so they are very expensive, and only made as a last resort when the application is of major significance to the applicant, and there appear to be good reasons for hoping the High Court will overturn the inspector's decision.

REMOVING AND VARYING PLANNING CONDITIONS

If your application is granted subject to a condition which you feel is impracticable or unacceptably restrictive, you have a number of options.

- You can choose to ignore the condition, and effectively challenge the local planning authority to take enforcement action against you (see Chapter 9).
- You can make an appeal (as above).
- You can make a planning application to remove or vary the condition.

If you appeal against a condition attached to a full planning application, the planning inspector has the authority not just to uphold the condition, but also to reject the entire application. However, if you make a new application to vary the condition, and then appeal against its refusal, the inspector cannot overturn the original permission.

MAKING A COMPLAINT TO THE LOCAL GOVERNMENT OMBUDSMAN

Making a complaint to the ombudsman is not a catch-all alternative to going through the usual appeals process. It is a separate procedure which should be used, not if you consider that your application might have been determined differently on planning grounds, but if you feel it has been significantly mishandled, or you have been treated unfairly.

Reasons for mishandling might include, for example, evidence that one or more of the councillors considering the application had a significant interest which they failed to declare, or that the committee clerk had wrongly recorded the decision of the committee, and the local planning authority had failed to right the error.

The right of appeal to the ombudsman does not apply only to applicants. Objectors to an application can also appeal if they have grounds (for example, if their objection was received by the local planning authority but not placed before the development control committee). So can neighbours, if the local planning authority had failed to carry out their statutory duty to consult, and the application has been approved to their detriment.

The ombudsman cannot alter the result of the planning decision, but he or she – there are a number of staff in the local government ombudsman's department – can call on the local planning authority to provide some other remedy, which could for example include the payment of compensation. The local planning authority is not forced to take the ombudsman's advice, but it needs to justify its decision publicly if it chooses not to do so.

OBJECTORS' APPEALS TO THE HIGH COURT

Although objectors do not have the right to appeal against approval of an application through the normal appeal process, they do have legal redress in some circumstances, and it is an option, albeit an expensive one, for an objector to appeal to the High Court.

KEY POINTS

✔ *When planning applications are received, a number of statutory bodies, other bodies such as local interest groups, and members of the public have an opportunity to comment on them.*

✔ *If your application prompts objections, you should consider them carefully. You could try to persuade the objectors to change their minds, or you could revise your application to take account of the objections.*

✔ *There is no additional fee for revising an application within a year of its first submission, whether it is considered and rejected, or withdrawn without formal consideration.*

✔ *Not all planning applications are considered by councillors. Some are determined by planning officers under their delegated powers*

✔ *If your application is considered at a development control meeting, it is up to you as applicant to find out when and where it is held, and to check the contents of the planning officer's report.*

✔ *As applicant, you have the right to have the case for approval of your application put to the committee, by yourself or by a councillor.*

✔ *If your application is rejected, or unacceptable conditions are placed on its acceptance, you can appeal to the Planning Inspectorate.*

✔ *If you feel your application was seriously mishandled, you can refer your complaint to the local government ombudsman.*

CHAPTER 7

Building *and* associated regulations

This chapter is concerned with the regulations that you need to observe when preparing for and carrying out building work. Once you have read it you should know:

- what the function is of the building control system
- where to obtain building control approval
- about the construction design and maintenance (CDM) process.

THE GENERAL SYSTEM OF BUILDING CONTROL

The building control system is currently regulated by the Building Act 1984, which consolidated much earlier legislation. Under that Act, sets of building regulations are issued at regular intervals on behalf of the Secretary of State for Transport, Local Government and the Regions, and it is these that specify how buildings should be designed and constructed. Over time, there has been a tendency for many specific points to be covered by guidance documents which supplement the regulations themselves.

The purpose of the system is twofold. First, it aims to regulate the construction process, and in particular:

- to ensure that everyone affected by the construction process – including builders, subcontractors, other employees of the enterprise, neighbours and passers-by – has their health, safety, welfare and convenience considered and secured as far as possible
- to ensure that fuel and power is conserved
- to prevent the misuse or contamination of water supplies.

Second, it aims to ensure that the building (whether it is new or altered) is erected in such a way that it will be safe after construction, and that some specific aspects such as access for disabled people are dealt with in accordance with the regulations.

Building control (BC) inspectors also have a duty to act over existing buildings which prove

73

to be defective or dangerous, and they oversee demolition works. Local authority building control inspectors may have other duties including ensuring safety at sports grounds and other open-air events, and inspecting cinemas and theatres.

Almost every new building, and every structural change to an existing building, needs to be given approval under the building regulations.

This process of control is separate from the development control practised by local planning authorities, although planners and building control inspectors liaise closely with each other.

WHO PROVIDES A BUILDING CONTROL SERVICE?

Since 1985, the building control process has been open to competition, and both private companies and local authorities provide building control services. As a developer, you can apply to be regulated either by the local authority building control service, or by a private Approved Inspector for Building Regulation Approval, who is authorised to regulate your type of development. Both types of service apply the same regulations, so they compete on cost, and on the level of service and convenience they provide to the users of their service.

THE PROCESS OF BUILDING CONTROL

There are several stages in the building control process.

First, the developer (or builder as the developer's agent) provides the building control inspector with information about the proposed development. Normally this information consists of full plans of the proposal, but if the development is small, it is sometimes adequate to send in a building notice which states what is proposed.

A fee is paid, usually on a sliding scale depending on the size of the proposal.

This information is reviewed for compliance with the regulations. The building control inspector normally consults the Fire Authority to ensure that the proposal conforms with fire regulations. As we have seen, the development control process allows considerable discretion, and there is some scope for discretion in applying the building regulations too: plans must be 'adequate' or 'suitable', but there are often several ways of achieving this. If the plans meet the regulation requirements, they will be passed, and if they fail to comply, amendments need to be made to ensure compliance.

The developer/builder must give the building control inspector statutory notice once the work begins, and the inspector is then responsible for inspecting, as necessary, while it is in progress, and for keeping a record of the inspections. Further notice has to be given before certain types and phases of work are carried out or completed; for example, before foundations, damp courses, drains and concrete work are covered up.

Once the work has been completed to the building control inspector's satisfaction, a completion certificate is issued.

TIMESCALE FOR BUILDING CONTROL

If you are planning a construction, it is advisable to consult a building control inspector at an early stage, so that you can ensure your plans are considered viable. Inspectors have a statutory five weeks to consider plans submitted to them. They must either pass or reject them within this time limit, but once you have made the formal application, you can start work at any time.

ACCESS FOR THE DISABLED

Among the issues covered by building control review of your plans, is access for the disabled: see page 60.

THE QUALITY OF MATERIALS

The agrément process, regulated by the British Board of Agrément, a quango, is responsible for controlling the quality of many building materials to ensure that they will be reliable and durable in use. It assesses materials using a combination of laboratory testing, site inspections and factory production control. Materials which meet the required standard are issued with an agrément certificate which effectively confirms that they comply with the requirements of the building regulations. Not all building materials require agrément certificates; some are quality controlled by British Standards, for example.

EXISTING BUILDINGS

The standards that are appropriate for new buildings are often not as easily applied to existing buildings, where materials that would not meet current standards have been used, and where the layout often makes it difficult to meet modern standards of accessibility and fire prevention. The building regulation system accepts this, and regulations are generally applied more flexibly to existing buildings than they are to new build (and especially to listed buildings, where there is a presumption against making external or internal changes). The baseline for building control inspectors is that any work which is carried out must not result in a less safe environment, but they need not always look for improvements on the previous situation.

BREACHES OF THE BUILDING REGULATIONS

It is a criminal offence to breach the building regulations, and if your building is erected without conformance to them, building control inspectors can issue a notice requiring you to alter it or, if necessary, demolish it. You may also be subject to a fine in the Magistrates Court.

DEMOLITION

Demolition work is also controlled by the Building Act, and if you wish to demolish a building, you must send the local authority a notice of your intention to demolish. (Planning permission is also required in some circumstances.) The local authority have six weeks to respond by issuing a 'Section 81' notice setting conditions which control the demolition process; if you do not receive a response within this time, you are entitled to go ahead. The local authority cannot refuse permission to demolish under these regulations, although they can refuse planning permission for demolition when this is required. The conditions might include, for example, making good any damage to adjoining buildings, disconnecting water, sewage and other services, removing rubble and making good the ground surface after demolition.

CONSTRUCTION DESIGN AND MANAGEMENT

Introduced in 1994, Construction Design and Management (CDM) is a separate set of regulations that set a framework for health and safety control of non-domestic construction projects. The regulations apply to most construction projects large and small, though there are some limited exemptions, and lesser requirements for some smaller projects: for instance, small-scale work in an office or shop that does not disrupt the normal activities.

The main purpose of these regulations is to determine clearly who is responsible for the health and safety of all those involved during construction work. Your obligations under these regulations are to appoint two individuals (or companies) to act as a 'planning supervisor' and a 'principal contractor', who are responsible for developing and enforcing a health and safety plan. You can appoint yourself to act as planning supervisor, but the person or body appointed as principal contractor must *be* a contractor. A health and safety file must be kept, and be available for inspection.

THE QUALITY MARK

If you are planning construction work, you may be interested in this new government scheme which is aimed at helping consumers identify honest, competent builders and allied traders. It is concerned with:

- ensuring builders have the technical skills necessary to do the job they tender for

- requiring builders to agree fair contracts covering the nature, extent and cost of work.

It is intended to be backed by an effective complaints system. The scheme was at the pilot stage in spring 2001, so it is not yet clear how wide take-up will be, or how well it will work.

KEY POINTS

✔ *Virtually all construction work, large and small, is subject to building regulations.*

✔ *It is essential to obtain building control approval for your plans before construction starts.*

✔ *Among the aspects covered by building control is access for the disabled.*

✔ *The building control process continues to operate throughout the construction phase.*

✔ *You need to inform the local authority of your intention to demolish a building under building regulations, even if you don't need planning permission to do so.*

✔ *You should also be aware of the CDM regulations which cover aspects of health and safety monitoring.*

Special considerations

This chapter looks at some of the planning issues which need to be considered in particular circumstances. It should make it clear to you:

- what impact archaeological remains could have on your development plans
- how being in a conservation area affects the planning process
- what you need to consider if your proposal involves a listed building or scheduled ancient monument
- what an Environmental Impact Assessment is, and when it is necessary
- what you need to consider if there are existing trees on your site
- how the planning process deals with telecommunications equipment
- how the planning process deals with outdoor advertisements.

ARCHAEOLOGY

There are around 600,000 archaeological sites recorded in England, and more than 16,000 monuments have been scheduled under the Ancient Monuments and Archaeological Areas Act 1979. These are not generally habitable buildings, which are covered under the listed buildings legislation discussed below. They vary from prehistoric earthworks to the foundations and ruins of medieval buildings. This is only part of our archaeological heritage. Many archaeological sites have yet to be discovered. You may know, or be able to discover quite easily, that archaeological remains exist on your proposed development site. Perhaps more disconcertingly, there is always a chance that significant archaeological remains which had not previously been known about will be discovered after you start construction work. This is equally true whether your site is in the centre of a historic city, in a new town, or a greenfield site in open country.

Archaeological remains will generally be an issue if you are planning new buildings, extensions, or any development (such as mineral excavation) which involves disturbing the soil. You have less need to worry if the work you are proposing is entirely above ground.

There is no single rule that applies when archaeological remains exist. A balance has to be struck between the need to conserve the past, and the need to develop for the future. It is not likely that you would be given permission to destroy a scheduled ancient monument (and conserving its setting is also a material planning issue), but if there are less significant remains on your site, its archaeology may be a constraining factor, but is unlikely to prevent you from developing.

If you know that your site is likely to harbour archaeological remains (as will very likely be the case, for example, if you are planning a sizeable development in a historic city centre) then you will need to discuss the situation with planning officers before you take your plans very far. They in turn will consult with archaeologists: both local authority experts and if necessary, English Heritage and its regional equivalents. If you don't do so, but the local authority is aware of potential remains on the site, then they will take the initiative. The presence of archaeological remains is rarely mentioned in local plans, but if yours is a known major site, it is quite likely that there will be existing policies or briefs covering it.

You may be asked to carry out an 'archaeological field evaluation'. This is not a full-scale 'dig': it is likely to consist of a survey of the ground, a check of existing records, and if the site is vacant, perhaps a 'trial trench' or two to see what is discovered. If it is apparent from the results of this evaluation that significant remains exist (or it was already known that this was the case), then the local planning authority will discuss with you how to proceed from that point.

The best option when developing a site is to preserve remains *in situ:* that is, simply to leave them be. It is not generally necessary to carry out a 'dig' and survey them in detail if this is a feasible solution. It can be achieved if you can locate your development on the site so as to leave the remains untouched, or if you are

able to design non-destructive foundations for any new buildings.

A second-best option is known as 'preservation by record': that is, the remains are dug up and reviewed, then detailed records are kept of what is found, but the remains themselves are destroyed.

If it is not clear whether the remains can be preserved *in situ*, then a dig is often required if the site is of archaeological significance. The local planning authority will make it a condition of your planning approval that this is done before your building work proper begins. Once the remains are uncovered by the dig, it may prove possible to adapt the plans so that they can be preserved.

It is usually your responsibility as developer to fund any dig that is a condition of your planning approval, though you may be able to obtain grants to assist with the cost, particularly if yours is a non-profit body. The local planning authority will prepare a brief which indicates what is required, and acts as the basis for an agreement between you as developer, the local planning authority and the archaeological contractor who carries out the dig. Archaeologists bid competitively for this work. The commitment usually extends to funding publication of the results of the dig.

It is particularly difficult if remains that were not anticipated are discovered after you have started excavation work. Perhaps your suburban site was once that of a Roman villa, for example. In this case, it is a question of advising the local planning authority and negotiating. If significant remains are found, it is possible for the Secretary of State to schedule them immediately, in order to give them protection. If it proves absolutely necessary, your planning permission can be revoked (in which case you are entitled to compensation), but this is rarely done. It is much better for everyone if a voluntary agreement is reached. You may have to postpone works while a dig is carried out, for example. It is possible for you to insure against this eventuality.

CONSERVATION AREA CONSENT

Conservation areas are outlined on page 33.

In a conservation area permission is needed:

- to demolish a building with a volume over 115 m³ (with some exceptions, and with the proviso that tighter rules may apply)
- to demolish a gate, fence, wall or railing over 1 metre high when next to a highway (including a public footpath or bridleway) or public open space, or over 2 metres high elsewhere.

It is necessary to apply to the local planning authority for 'conservation area consent' in these instances – a similar process to an application for planning permission. This permission applies only to demolition: there is no conservation area consent required for building works which are controlled through planning permission.

Often local planning authorities choose to apply stricter design guidelines in conservation areas than in less sensitive areas. These guidelines should be set out in local plans.

Article 4 directions

In order to control development to a higher standard in conservation areas, local planning authorities also have the right to remove some of the permitted development rights which would otherwise enable you to carry out small developments without planning permission. They do this by means of an 'Article 4 direction' which indicates the area affected and the development rights which have been restricted. The presumption is not that there is no development in the conservation area: it is simply that the development that does take place needs to be carefully controlled so as to ensure that it enhances the neighbourhood.

Article 4 directions can also be used to limit or control development in other ways. For instance, they may prevent you from carrying out work such as cladding the exterior of a building, or erecting a satellite dish, without applying for permission.

LISTED BUILDING CONSENT

Local planning authorities deal with granting listed building consent, which is required in addition to normal planning permission when work is being carried out on a listed building, and is also required for some work – particularly internal work – that does not need planning permission. However, applications for work on Grade I or II* buildings, or involving demolition, are generally referred to English Heritage for decision. There is currently no fee for a listed building application, whether or not planning permission is also being applied for. Applications are advertised in the same way as planning applications, both on site and in the press, with at least 21 days being allowed for consultation before they are determined.

The listing covers not only the building itself but other structures within its curtilage at the time it was listed, such as outbuildings and walls.

You must apply for listed building consent before making any material change to the outside or inside of the building which affects its character. To some extent it is a matter of judgment whether a change affects the building's character. For example, repainting woodwork in the same colour would not be a material change, but painting external woodwork in a different colour, if the building was part of a terrace of similarly painted buildings, would probably count as a material change, as would painting an external brick wall that had not previously been painted. Other work that would normally require consent includes:

- a change of material or style for the roof tiles
- replacement of existing windows
- the creation of an internal doorway where one did not previously exist
- the opening up of an older feature by removal of a more recent one.

When change of use is being considered for listed buildings, there is a presumption that to continue or resume the original use is the best option, but this is often not feasible, and an appropriate change of use is generally allowed when it will secure the future of the building.

Local authorities have powers to require owners to repair listed buildings if they fall into disrepair. They can issue two kinds of order: a 'repairs notice', and an 'urgent works notice'. They can repair unoccupied buildings themselves, and recover the cost from the owner; and if the owner does not act on an order to carry out repairs, the authority has the power to compulsorily purchase the building.

TELECOMMUNICATIONS EQUIPMENT

The erection of telecommunications equipment such as mobile phone masts can arouse a great deal of public controversy, particularly when there are perceived health risks. Local planning authorities are, however, limited to the usual planning grounds in deciding whether to allow applications for this type of development. In particular, government guidance is that they must not question whether the service to be provided is necessary, and they must – as is the case in other contexts – avoid restricting competition.

Government guidance is that telecommunications equipment can bring considerable benefits – for example, teleconferencing can reduce the need for business travel, and driver information systems can also have environmental benefits – so the presumption is that permissions will be granted where there is no overriding reason to refuse them.

Minor equipment such as satellite dishes can be treated in many cases as *de minimis*, or under the permitted development guidelines, and does not need planning permission. However, there are often tighter restrictions in conservation areas and for equipment on listed buildings, as was noted above.

ENVIRONMENTAL IMPACT ASSESSMENTS

It is good practice for any developer to take stock of the impact the proposed development will have on the environment. In some cases there is a statutory requirement for the developer to do so, through a process known as Environmental Impact Assessment (EIA), and to produce a formal document known as an environmental statement. Because these requirements apply mainly to heavy industrial developments, they are unlikely to affect small and medium-sized enterprises.

There is a statutory list of types of development which require an EIA, including:

- fuel-processing facilities, such as oil refineries
- many power stations
- radioactive waste handling facilities
- iron and steel works
- chemical works
- waste disposal incineration plants and landfill sites for special waste
- some transport-related developments.

Individual local planning authorities can also require EIAs to be prepared for other projects that are likely to have a significant effect on the environment.

The environmental statement needs to be drawn up in consultation with relevant authorities (such as English Nature and the Environment Agency), and must then accompany the planning application. Because these applications are usually complex, local planning authorities are allowed 16 weeks, rather than the usual eight to determine them.

TREES AND TPOS

All flora and fauna existing on your site deserve consideration, but you must pay particular attention to trees, as they have forms of statutory protection that do not apply to smaller plants.

Planning application forms usually ask if trees will be lost as a result of the application, and the location of existing trees needs to be marked on the accompanying site plan. It is permissible to fell trees without obtaining permission in advance unless they are either protected by a tree preservation order (TPO), or in a conservation area, in which case neither felling nor pruning without planning permission is allowed. However, trees should not be felled without careful consideration. If you are applying to develop a site which previously had tree cover, the local planning authority are likely to look for existing or replacement trees to feature in the landscape proposals for any part of the site which will not be built up.

If a tree is protected by a TPO, the presumption is that it should remain; but in some circumstances permission is given for TPO-protected trees to be removed, particularly if they are in a poor state. If this is agreed, it may be made a condition of the planning permission that a replacement tree is planted.

OUTDOOR ADVERTISEMENTS

'Outdoor' advertisements refer not just to billboards but also to advertisements on buildings, and to fly-posting, which is generally illegal (see Chapter 9).

Unless an outdoor advertisement falls within guidelines (see pages 30), it is necessary to apply for permission to display it. Local planning authorities do not have control over the subject matter of adverts, though other regulations do, of course, prevent the display of defamatory or obscene material. They do control their placement, their size, to some extent the materials of which they are constructed, and their lighting.

The considerations in determining these applications are how the advert will affect amenity and public safety. This is very much a question of context. A large and bright sign might be welcomed in a commercial area to which it contributes some colour and liveliness, but it would not be appropriate in a rural area. Poster hoardings are usually considered to be out of place except in commercial and industrial areas. However, a large poster which screens an ugly vacant site might be considered acceptable until the site is redeveloped.

Over 45 per cent of the land area of England and Wales is in designated 'areas of special control of advertisements', where 'deemed consent' is limited and stricter controls apply. Conservation areas are not automatically areas of special control, since many include town centres where large adverts are not inappropriate. Additional controls also apply to adverts placed on listed buildings (see above).

Local authorities have only a limited say over the design of adverts, as they do with buildings. In sensitive areas they can, for example, ask for corporate designs (such as McDonald's golden arches) to be modified, but government guidance is that they do not have the power to reject corporate designs simply because they dislike them.

All adverts are designed to attract attention, but there is a particular concern when attention may be drawn away from road signs and the like, which should take priority for safety reasons. Local planning authorities do have the right to reject, or ask for amendments to applications, which they consider unacceptable from a safety viewpoint.

KEY POINTS

✔ *Be prepared to fund an archaeological field evaluation or dig if your development site is thought likely to harbour archaeological remains.*

✔ *You can insure against the cost of unexpected archaeological finds hampering your development.*

✔ *You need conservation area consent to demolish any sizeable building in a conservation area.*

✔ *Be aware that permitted development rights can be limited by local planning authorities.*

✔ *Listed building consent is needed for internal as well as external work that alters the character of a listed building.*

✔ *Some environmentally sensitive development proposals require the production of an Environmental Impact Assessment.*

✔ *Planning consent is needed for outdoor advertisements which do not fit the 'deemed consent' guidelines.*

Enforcement action

This chapter aims to give an overview of the planning enforcement process. Once you have read it you should understand:

- what action a local planning authority can take against you
- what to do if you are threatened with enforcement action
- how to appeal against enforcement action
- what planning contraventions give rise to criminal offences
- how fly-posting is acted against.

WHEN ENFORCEMENT ACTION IS TAKEN

If you follow the correct procedures and apply for planning permission before undertaking a development, the subject of enforcement action will not concern you. However, you could find yourself facing enforcement action if:

- you did not apply for planning permission when it was required
- you failed to obtain planning permission, but have still gone ahead with the development
- your development is not in conformance with the application that was approved, or
- you have failed to observe a condition attached to planning consent.

Planning enforcement action can only be taken by your local planning authority (or in rare cases, the Secretary of State). It cannot be taken by anyone else who objects to your activity, although complaints from neighbours often prompt local planning authorities to start the enforcement process, and anyone who is adversely affected by your unauthorised activities may have other legal remedies against you.

ENFORCEMENT ACTIVITY

Only a small fraction of a local planning authority's work is concerned with enforcement, but planning authorities do use the full range of legal powers available to them.

In the last quarter of 2000, district-level planning authorities reported issuing 1,113 enforcement notices, 950 planning contravention notices, 294 breach of condition notices and 21 stop notices.

The courts granted five and refused three enforcement injunctions.

In the same period county-level planning authorities issued 28 enforcement notices and served three stop notices, 39 planning contravention notices and ten breach of condition notices.

TIME LIMITS

If a planning authority is to take enforcement action, it must do so within a fixed time after the unauthorised action takes place. The limits are:

- four years for building or engineering work
- four years for using a building as a single dwelling house without permission
- ten years for all other changes of use
- ten years for breaking planning conditions.

These limits do not apply, however, for unauthorised alterations to (or demolition of) listed buildings.

THE ENFORCEMENT PROCESS

The main planning enforcement process is intended to be used against developments (or changes of use) which have already taken place, rather than those that are planned for the future. If the local planning authority suspects that you are going to do something that is not authorised, they may apply to the county court or High Court for an injunction. The action you had been proposing to carry out might not have been a criminal offence, but it is a criminal offence to break the injunction; if the action had been a criminal offence (for example, demolishing a listed building without consent or felling a tree protected by a tree preservation order), the injunction would have the effect of increasing the likely penalties.

The steps below outline the more usual process that is taken when you have already carried out the action.

Investigating

The local planning authority will invariably start the enforcement process by investigating the situation. They will do this either because an officer or member of the council has become aware of the unauthorised development, or because someone else has brought it to their attention. They will normally do this through openly available means at first: for example, checking public records to find out the owner of the land involved, or visiting you to discuss the situation. If this does not provide the information they need, the local planning authority can use various legal powers, which include, at some points in the process, the right to enter privately owned land.

Requests for compliance

The general guidelines by which planning authorities work, state that they must not take enforcement action unnecessarily. If you have failed to obtain planning permission when you should have obtained it, your local planning authority should first contact you and, if it seems at all likely that it will be approved, advise you that you should apply for planning permission. They will not normally take any action against you if you then apply for, and obtain, permission.

Of course, there is no guarantee in this situation that you will obtain planning permission. If you apply and do not receive permission, or if the local planning authority advises you that you are unlikely to receive permission and suggests that you make changes before applying, if that is still necessary, then the situation is more difficult.

If it is reasonably practicable for you to meet the local planning authority's requirements, it is normally best to do so. If you do not feel you can meet their requirements, it is advisable first to meet the planning officer dealing with your case and discuss the situation. Although some local planning authorities now take a vigorous line on enforcement matters, most will do their best to avoid taking formal action, and if they are able to suggest practical solutions to the problem they will generally do so. (For example, they might know of an alternative site to which you could relocate your business.) They may also allow you a reasonably long period of time in which to make changes to your buildings or your activities, especially if you are providing valuable local employment.

If this does not resolve the problem, and you are still disinclined to comply, it is usually wise to obtain expert help. The type of help you require will depend on the kind of situation you face. For example:

- an architect or surveyor may be able to suggest how you can alter your building so as to enable it to meet the local planning authority's guidelines
- a planning consultant may be able to suggest arguments you can put to the local planning authority, or other ways in which you can meet their requirements
- a solicitor will advise you on the legal consequences of your action.

Legal notices

If the situation cannot be resolved informally, the local planning authority has the power to issue a number of different notices, to which you are legally obliged to respond.

Planning contravention notices

This notice is issued if the local planning authority has some proof that a breach of planning control has taken place, and is often used as a way of finding out more information. It can be issued to a landowner, an occupier or anyone else with an interest in the site (for instance, a mortgagee). It usually asks for specific information including the names and addresses of individuals involved, or dates when activity was started. It will give a time limit for responding (typically 28 days). Failure to respond to the notice is a criminal offence, as it is to knowingly or recklessly give misleading or false information.

Enforcement notices

An enforcement notice is the core notice the local planning authority uses to require you to comply with planning law. It does not have to issue a planning contravention notice before issuing an enforcement notice. The enforcement notice should state:

- what the unauthorised development is
- what the local planning authority requires you to do to correct the situation
- the time limit for doing it (which must be reasonable in the light of the action required)
- that there is the right of appeal to the Secretary of State.

This too can be issued to anyone with an interest in the site, and the person who is served, is placed under a duty to comply with it. If the local planning authority cannot find out who has an interest in the site, they can serve the notice by addressing it to the 'owner or occupier' and fixing it on the land.

To fail to respond to an enforcement notice is a criminal offence, as, once again, is the giving of false information.

Breach of condition notices

A breach of condition notice is sometimes issued instead of an enforcement notice when the recipient has failed to comply with a condition attached to planning permission. This is a faster process for the local planning authority because there is no right of appeal. (If you object to a condition on your planning permission, you need to appeal using the main planning appeal procedures.)

Stop notices

These are issued when the local planning authority requires an action to cease immediately. One might be used, for example, if your unauthorised business activities were causing unacceptable pollution in the neighbourhood. It is served either with, or following, an enforcement notice; it cannot be served without one. Although you can appeal against the enforcement notice, that does not prevent the stop notice from having immediate effect.

Direct action

If you do not comply with a legal notice, the local planning authority has the right to take legal action against you. The maximum summary penalty for contravening an enforcement or stop notice is £20,000, so this threat should be taken very seriously. The local planning authority also has the right to carry out the work required itself if you do not do so. It can enter onto privately owned land for this purpose, and can charge the owner of the land for the work that is carried out.

APPEALING AGAINST ENFORCEMENT ACTION

If the type of notice with which you have been served allows an appeal, you may find it worthwhile to make the appeal to the Secretary of State. The appeal has the effect of stopping the clock on enforcement action, so even if your appeal is refused you will still have the original time limit within which to act.

An appeal need not be made by the person or body on whom the notice was served; it can be made by anyone with an interest in the land, so if the notice is served on the landowner and you are the occupier but not the landowner, you still have the right of appeal.

Appeals will only be granted if you can show proper grounds for making the appeal. The allowable grounds are:

- that planning permission ought to be granted for the activity or development
- that the alleged breach has not actually occurred
- that although the alleged action has occurred, it is not a breach of planning control
- that the breach is immune from enforcement action
- that the notice was not served correctly
- that the action required by the notice is excessive in comparison with the breach
- or that insufficient time has been allowed in the notice for the action to be carried out.

Note that it is not an adequate ground for appeal that you will find it difficult to do as the notice requires. Similarly, if the notice allows a reasonable amount of time, but you feel you need further time in order to relocate your activities, this is not an adequate ground for appeal.

It is advisable to enlist expert help if you wish to appeal against enforcement action.

CRIMINAL OFFENCES

To carry out unauthorised development is not always a criminal offence. However, if you ignore a legal notice requiring you to comply with planning requirements, this is a criminal offence, even if your original action was not.

Some particular actions against planning law are also criminal offences, and you can be prosecuted for doing them without any need for further action:

- felling a tree protected by a tree preservation order, or any tree in a conservation area, without permission
- demolishing a building in a conservation area without permission
- demolishing a listed building without permission.

Although enforcement notices of most kinds can be served on anyone with an interest in the land, only the person or body who actually did the unauthorised action is liable to be prosecuted.

FLY-POSTING

It is always an offence to fly-post: that is, to stick adverts on another person's (or public) property, or on street furniture (lamp posts, bus shelters and so on) without authorisation. Fly-posting is controlled by the Town and Country Planning Act 1990 and the Town and Country Planning (Control of Advertisements) Regulations 1992. These specify fines of up to £1,000 for unauthorised fly-posting; and if you continue to display the notices after conviction, you can be fined a further £100 per day.

The fine is levied either on the owner or occupier of the land (unless they can prove the notice was displayed without their knowledge or consent) or the person whose goods, trade, business or other concerns received publicity from the advert.

As an alternative to prosecuting, the local authority can give two days' notice to the person responsible for the advert, if they can be identified, and then if it has not been removed, proceed to obliterate or remove it. No notice needs to be given if the person responsible cannot be identified, or for adverts on street furniture or on the highway (which are covered in the Highways Act 1980). In London, the London Local Authorities Act 1995 allows London boroughs not only to remove posters, but also to recover their costs in doing so.

KEY POINTS

✔ *Enforcement action against breaches of planning control has to be initiated within time limits, or the development or activity becomes immune from action.*

✔ *Enforcement action is generally only taken when the local planning authority and the developer have failed to come to an amicable agreement.*

✔ *It is a criminal offence to fail to respond to most types of formal enforcement action.*

✔ *If you do not carry out actions required of you, the local planning authority has the right to do so on your behalf.*

✔ *There is a right of appeal against most types of enforcement notice.*

✔ *The local authority has wide powers to ensure that fly posters are removed or obliterated.*

CHAPTER 10

You neighbours; your future

This chapter explains how to keep abreast of what is being planned in your local neighbourhood, your area and your region. Once you have read it you should be aware:

- how information about planning applications is made available
- what rights of information you have about larger projects
- how to object to planning proposals
- how to comment on local plans and district plans.

WHAT YOUR NEIGHBOURS DO

Plans in your immediate neighbourhood may have a significant effect on your business and those who work in it. It is important that you be aware what is being proposed, and that you object in good time if what is proposed may be to your detriment.

Although you do not have a great deal of control over what your neighbours do on their own property, you do have certain rights which affect what they can do. These include:

- **Rights of way.** Roads, footpaths and bridle paths which are public rights of way cannot be stopped up or diverted without a legal order.

- **Rights of support.** You may have a right for the foundations of your buildings to be supported from adjacent land, a right which may become important should your neighbour propose works that would involve moving earth close to your property boundary. Whether you have such a right depends on the circumstances but, in general, the longer your building has been supported by the adjoining land, the more likely it is that you have a right of support.

- **Rights of light and air.** These are limited rights and do not give you an automatic right to the amount of light or flow of air that you currently receive.

You also have the right to a degree of knowledge about your neighbour's plans, once these become the subject of a planning application, and to consultation on planning grounds.

You do *not* have rights to insist that your neighbour does not act in any way that affects you for the worse. If your neighbour's proposed development affects the value of your own land or buildings, or otherwise affects your activities in ways which are not proper matters for consideration by the planning system, that is unfortunately your bad luck and there is little that you can do about it. However, it may be that case law under the Human Rights Act will serve to extend your rights in this type of situation.

FINDING OUT ABOUT PROPOSALS

The local planning authority has a statutory duty to publicise planning applications it receives, but of course, that only comes into play when a formal application is submitted, and this may be some way down the path of development. It is obviously better if you are aware of potential developments which might affect you at an earlier stage. You might, for example, learn about them through local chambers of commerce or other commercial organisations, or by formal or informal contacts with your neighbours, and it is always worth cultivating your channels of communication. It may seem unlikely that you will be able to influence your neighbours' development proposals, and indeed they probably will not amend them to your advantage, and against their own, unless they absolutely have to, but most developers see the advantages in keeping on good terms with their neighbours, and if they can orient their proposals in a way which benefits you without harming themselves, this may be a real advantage to you.

In addition, your knowledge will help you plan your own activities: for example, reorganising your office so that staff who work extensively over the telephone are as far as possible from likely building works, or planning a new extension in an area of your site where it will not sit awkwardly with your neighbour's proposals.

It is certainly important that you learn about planning applications once they are submitted. As well as looking out for site notices, it is worth checking the local paper for advertisements from the local planning authority. Once you become aware of an application, you have the right to review the proposals in detail at the local planning authority's office. If the application is likely to have a major impact on you, you may find it worthwhile to ask an architect, surveyor or planning consultant to review it for you and make comments. Of course, you should take careful note of the deadline for submitting objections.

OBJECTING TO PLANNING APPLICATIONS

You can express your support for planning applications as well as your objections to them, but understandably you may be more anxious to do the latter. The best way to do so is to write to the local planning authority. It is not essential for letters to be typed, but a well-produced and neatly laid-out letter is always likely to make the best impression. Keep your letter reasonably brief, and try to ensure that the points you make are valid in planning terms. Valid objections might be, for instance:

- The site is in an area that is unsuitable for the proposed type of use, either because of the pattern of existing uses, or because it is too poorly served in transport terms. (If you are aware that it is designated for other uses in the local plan, you can emphasise this point too.)
- The proposal will generate an unacceptable amount of traffic on local roads that are not equipped to carry it.
- The proposal has inadequate parking provision, and public parking spaces in local streets are already occupied almost all the time.

- The proposed activities will generate an unacceptable level of noise, air or water pollution.
- The building design is out of keeping with the area.
- The proposed building is too large for the site and overshadows or overlooks neighbouring buildings to an unacceptable degree.
- The proposed development will increase the flood risk on other sites, perhaps including your own.

Try to make your comments as impersonal as possible. Focus on the proposals and what is acceptable or unacceptable about them, not on the likely effect on your business.

If you have several points to make, separate them out clearly. Bear in mind that your letter may be summarised for inclusion in the planning officer's report and that objections are not confidential. Before the application is discussed in committee, the applicant will be able to find out what comments have been made, and who has made them.

We gave advice in Chapter 6 about lobbying council members in order to gain support for your own planning application. The same advice holds if you wish to press your objection to someone else's planning application. You can contact any relevant councillor, by phone, letter, fax or e-mail, make your points (including, informally, more personal points than you might choose to make in a formal letter of objection) and if you think it warranted, ask him or her to visit your premises so that you can show exactly how the proposals will affect you.

You may not be allowed to speak at the development control committee meeting at which the application is discussed, although this situation may change under Human Rights legislation, but you can ask a councillor to make points to the committee on your behalf, and you do have the right to attend the committee meeting. (See Chapter 6 for how to find out when and where the meeting will be held.)

Objectors are not automatically told about the results of planning applications, although there are some initiatives to ensure that they are kept better informed. If you attend the development control meeting, you will know (or at least get a good sense of) the outcome. If not, you can find out by phoning the local planning authority shortly after the meeting takes place.

As an objector, you do not have any right of appeal if a planning application is approved against your will. However, if you believe that the planning system has been operated unjustly – for example, that the local planning authority failed in its duty of consultation – then you can turn to the local government ombudsman, or take legal action in the High Court. (See Chapter 6 for details of how to do this.)

FINDING OUT ABOUT MAJOR PROJECTS

When a small development is proposed, relatively few people and organisations are generally affected by it; but a large development such as the redevelopment of an empty site to provide a major shopping centre, or a mixed-use development with shopping, housing and leisure uses, or a major new road will affect a wide variety of people. For example:

- The development may affect property values over a relatively wide area.

- The development is likely to provide new competition for businesses.
- The development may lead to changes in the road system, and will almost certainly affect traffic patterns.
- The development may change patterns of economic behaviour, in less obvious as well as immediately obvious ways. Not only shops, but other businesses which attract passing trade, or which depend even slightly on on-site advertising, may notice the effect of changes in shopping trends, travel-to-work routes and so on.

The government recognises that for these and similar reasons, many people have a legitimate interest in the likely pattern of major development in their area. The public do, of course, have a right to comment on structural planning proposals (see below), and on formal planning applications, but their interest in a particular development is likely to be more detailed than the structure plan provides for, and to exist long before the planning application comes up for determination.

The need for the public to know what is proposed has to be balanced, however, against the right of the developer to commercial confidentiality. The government's guidelines are based on the principle that 'At all stages members of the public have the right to expect the promoter to observe a general policy of candour and openness in respect of proposed developments which may affect the quality of life in the area generally, and the value of local properties particularly'. However, the type of information that will be released is shaped by the needs of confidentiality. It will not generally include details of land transactions, for example, which are accepted as confidential; but it could include details about the intended mix of uses on the site, before the stage at which formal planning permission is applied for.

The DTLR has issued a code of practice about the release of information on major development proposals, and the relevant local planning authority should be able to advise you on the information that is publicly available on major proposals in their area. If developers do make information available, it is permissible for them to make a charge for providing it.

CONSULTATION ON LOCAL AND STRUCTURE PLANS

We outlined in Chapter 2 the framework of planning policy which includes structure plans at the county, or equivalent level, and local plans at the level of the local planning authority area. These plans are drawn up via a process which includes extensive public consultation. Whether or not you are intending to put forward planning applications yourself, you will find the content of these plans is important to you. It will determine, for example:

- how wider patterns of commercial activity will develop in the area
- what housing is planned, and what new markets might emerge as a result
- how the transport infrastructure will develop
- what uses will be acceptable both in broad areas and on specific sites.

You have the opportunity to influence these decisions (albeit in a small way) by making representations at the right time. If you have an interest in a site which you wish to develop, this process can be the most crucial part of the entire planning cycle.

The plan process

The process of drawing up a structure plan or local plan, and of making amendments to it (which is more usual, since most planning authorities now have plans in place), normally begins with a period of *pre-deposit consultation*. At this stage the planning authority will not have finalised its proposals, and the consultation tends to focus on key issues – for example, whether a bypass is needed, or how much new housing or industry should be provided for, and where – in order to gain a sense of the public attitude to them. The extent and length of this consultation is at the discretion of the planning authority.

The draft plan is then drawn up, and is put on *deposit*: that is, it is made publicly available, for example in libraries and council offices. At the same time, the planning authority have to outline what consultation they have undertaken, and what feedback, they received. The deposit of the plan is followed by a statutory six-week period during which objections can be lodged.

The planning authority is obliged to consider all the objections and representations it receives. It must make available a schedule of them, and make the objectors' statements available for viewing if required. It may choose to negotiate with objectors, and to revise the plan to take account of their comments, in which case the objectors have the opportunity to withdraw their objections. If objections are not withdrawn, they automatically go forward to be considered by the planning inspector.

If changes are made as a result of this process, the revised plan goes on deposit, and there is a further six-week period for objections.

The next stage is a public inquiry, heard by a planning inspector who is appointed by the Secretary of State. The public and organisations, who have previously made representations or objections, can make written representations to the public inquiry, or give oral evidence at it.

Following the inquiry, the inspector publishes a report with recommendations to the planning authority. The authority must consider the report and make its deliberations publicly available within eight weeks of its receipt. It must either modify the published plan to take account of the inspector's recommendations, or if it chooses not to take any of the recommendations on board, produce a statement of its reasons for not accepting them.

There is then a further six-week period for objections either to proposed modifications, or to a decision by the planning authority not to accept a recommendation in the inspector's report. If further changes are made in the light of this consultation, the process is repeated otherwise the plan is adopted.

How to comment on plan proposals

Your comments on, or objections to, the plan must be put in writing. They must be submitted within the time limit, and they must make it clear what is being objected to and why. Of course, the reason for objecting must be one that is valid in planning terms. The fact that you would prefer a development not to take place is not a valid reason, but an argument that insufficient land has been allocated for employment purposes would be valid, for example.

If you wish, you can suggest changes to meet the objection: so, for example, the objection that insufficient land has been allocated for employment purposes could be accompanied with a suggestion that a specific area be given this use allocation.

If you choose to appear at a local inquiry, this must be at your own expense. You need to pay your own out-of-pocket expenses, and even if the plan is modified to take account of your objections, no costs are awarded to or against anyone. You can be legally represented if you wish, but this too must be at your expense. You and other objectors can also join together to make joint representations to the inquiry. You may also be able to obtain assistance through the Planning Aid initiative (see page 43).

COMMENTING ON PLANNING BRIEFS

We outlined in Chapter 2 the process of drawing up planning briefs for specific sites. These too are normally subject to a consultation process, and you can, if you wish, make representations. Since planning briefs determine in some detail what is to be permitted on a specific site, you will certainly want to make representations if you are considering development on the site, and may well want to do so if you are a near neighbour, or otherwise likely to be affected by the development.

The process of consultation for planning briefs is much less formal, and is conducted entirely by the local planning authority without the intervention of an inspector. If the local planning authority knows of your interest in the site, they will normally contact you and invite you to make comments, so it is worth letting the local planning authority know of your interest. Otherwise, you may learn that the planning brief is being prepared through informal channels, through the local paper, or by checking the minutes of council meetings.

KEY POINTS

✔ *If your immediate neighbours are likely to develop their land, you need to be aware of how your rights help to determine what will and will not be permitted.*

✔ *It is best to find out about planning proposals as early as possible, before the stage of a formal planning application, but it is also important to keep an eye on planning applications so that you do not find out about them too late to have any influence.*

✔ *Objections to planning applications can only be made on valid planning grounds.*

✔ *The government's code of conduct should enable you to find out additional information about major development proposals which may affect you.*

✔ *Whether you plan to develop or not, consider the advantages of making representations when the local and structure plans for your area are being revised.*

✔ *Ensure your local planning authority know of your interest in any major sites likely to be developed, so you can be consulted if they draw up a planning brief.*

Glossary

agrément certificate a certificate confirming the quality and suitability of building materials

Article 4 direction a requirement by local planning authorities for stricter controls (for example, on permitted design types) to apply to development in sensitive areas

'bad neighbour' uses heavy industrial and other noisy, smelly or polluting land uses which require special consideration

building control the process of regulating the construction of buildings (and some other issues, such as demolition), which is separate from development control

buildings of local interest buildings designated by the local planning authority as of particular interest, which are subject to some additional planning controls

conservation area an area designated by the local planning authority as of special architectural or historic interest, in which additional controls are placed on land-use development

Construction Design and Management (CDM) regulations covering the health and safety of non-domestic construction projects

county matters the subject of planning applications that are determined by county-level planning authorities (primarily mineral extraction and waste disposal sites)

curtilage the land surrounding a building, which is considered with it in planning terms

deemed consent the process by which (mostly minor) types of development, set out in government regulations, are assumed to have approval without the need to apply for planning permission

delegated decisions the process by which officers of the local planning authority determine planning applications without their being referred to a committee of members

de minimis the rule for changes of very minor scale, that do not require specific planning permission

DENI Department of the Environment for Northern Ireland

development control the process of considering planning applications

development control committee the committee (made up of members of the local planning authority) that determines most planning applications

district matters the subject of the majority of planning applications that are determined by district-level planning authorities

DTLR Department of Transport, Local Government and the Regions

enforcement action the process by which local planning authorities deal with breaches of planning law

Environmental Impact Assessment a statutorily required assessment of the environmental impact of certain classes of major development

green belt an area surrounding a built-up area (normally a city or conurbation) within which there is a presumption that development will not take place

lawful development certificate a certificate issued by an local planning authority confirming that an existing or planned development or use does not need additional planning permission

listed building a building listed by the Secretary of State for its architectural or historic interest, subject to additional development restrictions

local list a list of buildings of interest, which are not listed buildings as defined above, that is compiled by the local planning authority rather than the Secretary of State

local plan an outline of current and planned land-use patterns and other development issues, drawn up on a district scale

LPA local planning authority

OPP outline planning permission, agreeing the general principle of development, but requiring to be turned into full planning permission before development takes place

permitted development the process by which certain relatively minor types of development, set out in government regulations, are permitted to go ahead without the need to apply for planning permission

planning agreement or obligation a commitment by a developer to perform certain actions, or not, as the case may be, or to make a payment towards some type of facility, as a condition of obtaining planning permission

planning brief guidance issued by the local planning authority on the type of development they expect to see on a specific site

planning condition a condition attached to a grant of planning permission

PPG planning policy guidance: as embodied in a set of documents issued by the DTLR (and by regional legislative bodies)

reserved matters matters not covered in OPP (see above), which need to be agreed before full planning permission is granted

RPG regional planning guidance, drawn up by regional planning forums and providing a regional framework for planning decisions

simplified planning zone a designated area within which the normal requirements for permission are relaxed (in specified ways) to encourage development

SPG supplementary planning guidance drawn up by local planning authorities

Section 106 agreement a planning agreement or obligation (see above)

structure plan an outline of current and planned land-use patterns and other development issues, drawn up on a county (or equivalent) scale

Reference Material

FURTHER READING

Planning law

Among the legislation of particular importance in a land-use and planning context are:

Building Act 1984

Control of Advertisements Regulations 1992

Fire Precautions Act 1971

Highways Act 1980

Planning and Compensation Act 1991

Planning (Listed Buildings and Conservation Areas) Act 1990

Planning (Listed Buildings and Conservation Areas) (Scotland) Act 1997

Planning (Northern Ireland) Order 1991

Town and Country Planning Act 1990

Town and Country Planning (General Permitted Development) Order 1995

Town and Country Planning (Scotland) Act 1997

Town and Country Planning (Environmental Impact Assessment) (England and Wales) Regulations 1999

Use Classes Order 1987

Planning policy guidance

The following documents (all published by The Stationery Office, and available on the DTLR's website) provide guidance on planning policy in England. There are similar documents for Wales and Scotland: details are available from The Stationery Office, or from the Scottish Parliament and Welsh Assembly websites. All PPGs are subject to regular review and updating.

PPG1: General Policy and Principles

PPG2: Green Belts

PPG3: Housing

PPG4: Industrial and Commercial Development and Small Firms

PPG6: Town Centres and Retail Developments

PPG8: Telecommunications

PPG11: Regional Planning

PPG 12: Development Plans

PPG13: Transport

PPG 16: Archaeology and Planning

PPG18: Enforcing Planning Control

PPG19: Outdoor Advertisement Control

PPG21: Tourism

PPG 22 Renewable Energy

PPG23: Planning and Pollution Control

PPG24: Planning and Noise

PPG25: Development and Flood Risk

Other official documents

Most of these documents are available, in full or summary form, on government websites.

DETR/National Assembly for Wales (1997) *Planning: A Guide for Householders,* London: DETR (free)

DETR (1998) *Modernising Planning,* London: DETR

DETR (1998) *Planning and Development Briefs: A Guide to Better Practice,* London: DETR

DETR (1999) *The Economic Consequences of Planning to the Business Sector,* London: DETR

DETR (1999) *Local Plans and Unitary Development Plans: A Guide to Procedures,* London: DETR

DETR (1999) *Code of Practice on the Dissemination of Information during Major Infrastructure Developments,* London: DETR

DETR (2000) *The Control of Fly-Posting: A Good Practice Guide,* London: DETR

DETR (2000) *Mediation in the Planning System,* London: DETR

DETR (2000) *By Design, Urban Design in the Planning System: Towards Better Practice,* London: Thomas Telford (and free summary from DETR)

DETR (2000) *Planning Permission: A Guide for Business,* London: DETR

DETR (2001) *Statutory and Non-Statutory Consultation Report,* London: DETR

Health & Safety Executive (n/d) *Having Construction Work Done? Duties of Clients under the Construction (Design and Management) Regulations 1994,* London: HSE

HM Govt (1994) *Sustainable Development: The UK Strategy,* London: HMSO

HM Govt (1998) *A New Deal For Transport: Better for Everyone,* White Paper, London: HMSO

Scottish Executive (2000) National Planning Policy Guidance, *'The Planning System'* (Draft), Edinburgh: Scottish Executive.

Welsh Office (1999) *Planning Policy, First Revisions,* Planning Guidance (Wales), Cardiff: Welsh Office.

Other documents

The fullest summary of planning law is provided by Sweet and Maxwell's *Encyclopaedia of Planning Law and Practice*, which comprises six volumes and is regularly updated. Your local reference library should have a copy.

Contact addresses

Association of Building Engineers
Lutyens House, Billing Brook Road
Weston Favell
Northampton NN3 8NW
Tel. 01604 404121
Fax 01604 784220
www.abe.org.uk

British Property Federation
35 Catherine Place
London SW1E 6DY
Tel. 020 7828 0111
Fax 020 7834 3442

Business in the Community (England)
8-9 Stratton Street
London W1X 5FD
Tel. 0870 600 2482
Fax 020 7253 1877

Business in the Community (Wales)
6th Floor, Empire House
Mount Stuart Square
Cardiff CF1 6DN
Tel. 029 20 483348
Fax 029 20 461513

Commission for Architecture and the Built Environment
The Tower Building, 11 York Road
London SE1 7NX
Tel. 020 7960 2400
Fax 020 7960 2444
www.cabe.org.uk

Confederation of British Industry
Centre Point, 103 New Oxford Street
London WC1A 1DU
Tel. 020 7379 7400
Fax 020 7240 0988

Department of Transport, Local Government and the Regions
Eland House, Bressenden Place
London SW1E 5DU
Tel. 020 7944 3000
www.detr.gov.uk

Department for Culture, Media and Sport
2-4 Cockspur Street
London SW1Y 5DH
Tel. 020 7211 6200
www.heritage.gov.uk

English Heritage
Fortress House, 23 Savile Row
London W1X 1AB
Tel. 020 7973 3000
Fax 020 7973 3001

Health & Safety Executive
Information Centre, Broad Lane
Sheffield S3 7HQ
Tel. 08701 545550
www.hse.gov.uk

WALES & WEST DIVISION
Covers Wales and the unitary authorities of Cornwall, Devon, Somerset, North West Somerset, Bath and North East Somerset, Bristol, South Gloucestershire, Gloucestershire, Hereford & Worcester, Shropshire and Staffordshire.

Government Buildings, Phase 1
Ty Glas, Llanishen
Cardiff CF14 5SH
Tel. 029 2026 3000
Fax 029 2026 3120

Inter City House
Mitchell Lane
Victoria Street
Bristol BS1 6AN
Tel. 01179 886000
Fax 01179 262998

The Marches House
Midway
Newcastle-under-Lyme ST5 1DT
Tel. 01782 602300
Fax 01782 602400

HOME COUNTIES DIVISION

Covers the counties of Bedfordshire, Berkshire, Buckinghamshire, Cambridgeshire, Dorset, Essex (except London Boroughs in Essex), Hampshire, Hertfordshire, Isle of Wight, Norfolk, Suffolk and Wiltshire.

14 Cardiff Road
Luton LU1 1PP
Tel. 01582 444200
Fax 01582 444320

Priestley House, Priestley Road
Basingstoke RG24 9NW
Tel. 01256 404000
Fax 01256 404100

39 Baddow Road
Chelmsford CM2 0HL
Tel. 01245 706200
Fax 01245 706222

LONDON & SOUTH EAST DIVISION

Covers the counties of Kent, Surrey, East Sussex and West Sussex, and all London Boroughs.

St Dunstans House
201-211 Borough High Street
London SE1 1GZ
Tel. 020 7556 2100
Fax 020 7556 2200

3 East Grinstead House
London Road
East Grinstead RH19 1RR
Tel. 01342 334200
Fax 01342 334222

MIDLANDS DIVISION

Covers the counties of West Midlands, Leicestershire, Northamptonshire, Oxfordshire, Warwickshire, Derbyshire, Lincolnshire and Nottinghamshire.

McLaren Building, 35 Dale End
Birmingham B4 7NP
Tel. 0121 607 6200
Fax 0121 607 6349

5th Floor, Belgrave House
1 Greyfriars
Northampton NN1 2BS
Tel. 01604 738300
Fax 01604 738333

1st Floor, The Pearson Building
55 Upper Parliament Street
Nottingham NG1 6AU
Tel. 01159 712800
Fax 01159 712802

YORKSHIRE & NORTH EAST DIVISION

Covers the counties and unitary authorities of Hartlepool, Middlesbrough, Redcar and Cleveland, Stockton-on-Tees, Durham, Hull, North Lincolnshire, North East Lincolnshire, East Riding, York, North Yorkshire, Northumberland, West Yorkshire, Tyne & Wear, and the metropolitan Boroughs of Barnsley, Doncaster, Rotherham and Sheffield.

Marshalls Mill, Marshall Street
Leeds LS11 9YJ
Tel. 0113 283 4200
Fax 0113 283 4296

Sovereign House, 110 Queen Street
Sheffield S1 2ES
Tel. 0114 291 2300
Fax 0114 291 2379

Arden House, Regent Centre
Regent Farm Road
Gosforth
Newcastle-upon-Tyne NE3 3JN
Tel. 0191 202 6200
Fax 0191 202 6300

NORTH WEST DIVISION

Covers the counties of Cheshire, Cumbria, Greater Manchester, Lancashire and Merseyside.

Grove House
Skerton Road
Manchester M16 0RB
Tel. 0161 952 8200
Fax 0161 952 8222

Victoria House
Ormskirk Road
Preston PR1 1HH
Tel. 01772 836200
Fax 01772 836222

SCOTLAND
Covers all the Scottish unitary authorities and
island councils.

Belford House
59 Belford Road
Edinburgh EH4 3UE
Tel. 0131 247 2000
Fax 0131 247 2121

375 West George Street
Glasgow G2 4LW
Tel. 0141 275 3000
Fax 0141 275 3100

Offshore Safety Division
Lord Cullen House
Fraser Place
Aberdeen AB25 3UB
Tel. 01224 252500
Fax 01224 252662

Institution of Civil Engineers
1-7 Great George Street
London SW1P 3AA
Tel. 020 7222 7722
Fax 020 7722 7500
www.ice.org.uk

Institute of Field Archaeologists
University of Reading
2 Earley Gate
P O Box 239
Reading RG6 6AU
Tel. 0118 931 6446
Fax 0118 931 6448
www.archaeologists.net

LOCAL GOVERNMENT OMBUDSMEN
There are three local government ombudsmen
in England. Each of them deals with
complaints from different parts of the
country:

London boroughs north of the River Thames
(including Richmond), Essex, Kent, Surrey,
Suffolk, East and West Sussex:

Mr E B C Osmotherly CB
Local Government Ombudsman
21 Queen Anne's Gate
London SW1H 9BU
Tel. 020 7915 3210
Fax 020 7233 0396

The West Midlands (except Coventry City),
Staffordshire, Shropshire, Cheshire,
Derbyshire, Nottinghamshire, Lincolnshire
and the north of England (except the Cities of
York and Lancaster):

Mrs P A Thomas
Local Government Ombudsman
Beverley House
17 Shipton Road
York YO30 5FZ
Tel. 01904 663200
Fax 01904 663269

London boroughs south of the River Thames
(except Richmond); the Cities of York,
Lancaster and Coventry); and the rest of
England, not included in the areas of Mr
Osmotherly and Mrs Thomas:

Mr J R White
Local Government Ombudsman
The Oaks No 2
Westwood Way
Westwood Business Park
Coventry CV4 8JB
Tel. 024 7669 5999
Fax 024 7669 5902

THE PLANNING INSPECTORATE

Customer Support Unit
Room 3/15 Eagle Wing
Temple Quay House
2 The Square
Temple Quay
Bristol BS1 6PN
Tel. 0117 372 6372
Fax 0117 372 8782
www.planning-inspectorate.gov.uk

Welsh Office (for planning appeals in Wales)
Cathays Park
Cardiff CF1 3NQ
Tel. 029 20 823288
Fax 020 20 823356
www.building-control.org.uk

Royal Institution of Chartered Surveyors
12 Great George Street
Parliament Square
London SW1P 3AD
Tel. 020 7222 7000
Fax 020 7222 9430

Royal Town Planning Institute
41 Botolph Lane
London EC3R 8DL
Tel. 020 7929 9494
Main Fax. 020 7929 9490
www.rtpi.org.uk
email: online@rtpi.org.uk

Rural Development Commission
Dacre House, 19 Dacre Street
London SW1H 0DH
Tel. 020 7340 2900
Fax 020 7340 2911

The Scottish Office
The Secretary and Head of Department
Development Department
Victoria Quay
Edinburgh EH6 6QQ
Fax 0131 244 0785

Town and Country Planning Association
17 Carlton House Terrace
London SW1Y 5AS
Tel. 020 7930 8903
Fax 020 7930 3280
www.tcpa.org.uk

Welsh Development Agency
Principality House, The Friary
Cardiff CF1 4AA
Tel. 0845 777 5577

Index